MOROCCO-KOREA COOPERATION

Contemporary Partnership and Future Insights

MOROCCO-KOREA COOPERATION
Contemporary Partnership and Future Insights

First Print	02 May, 2025
First Edition	02 May, 2025

Author	John Gyun Yeol Park et al.
Publisher	Jong-Jun Chae
Published by	Korea Studies Information Co., Ltd.
Address	230 Hoedong-gil, Munpyeong-dong, Paju-si, Gyeonggi-do, Republic of Korea
Tel	+82-3.1-908-3181 (Main)
Fax	+82-31-908-3189
Email	ksibook1@kstudy.com
Reg. No.	Jeilsan-115 (June 19, 2000)
ISBN	979-11-7318-394-2 93300

MOROCCO-KOREA COOPERATION

Contemporary Partnership and Future Insights

Edited by **John Gyun Yeol Park**

President, Korea Association for Public Value
Professor, Gyeongsang National University, ROK

CONTENTS

FORWARD

H.E. Dr. Chafik RACHADI,
Ambassador of His Majesty the King of Morocco to the Republic of Korea

It is a great honor for me, in my capacity as Ambassador of His Majesty the King of Morocco to the Republic of Korea, to present this book, a compilation of research papers from the conference on "Mutual Cooperation between Morocco and Korea: Past, Present, and Future," organized by the Korean Association for Public Value and hosted by Seoul National University of Education (Seoul, SNUE, December 13, 2024).

At a pivotal moment in global interchange, this conference provided a platform to discuss matters related to economic, political and cultural cooperation between Morocco and Korea, as the event brought together specialists from different backgrounds and universities. The invited experts provided us with both food for thought and topics for enthusiastic debate. These experts hailed from various institutions, including Seoul National University of Education and Gyeongsang National University -Korea-; Harvard University and Western Illinois University -USA-; University of Waterloo -Canada-; Zhengzhou Normal University -China-; University of Philippines -Philippines-; Stamford International University -Thailand-; Dhaka University -Bangladesh-; and many others.

As will be evident throughout the book, the lecturers addressed the following key topics:

- *Korea's PKO Activities in Moroccan Sahara and Their Significance;*
- *Korea's PKO activities, including Korea Medical Unit, in the Moroccan Sahara;*
- *International support for the Moroccan Sahara;*
- *International Cooperation in the Moroccan Sahara and the potential of the Autonomy Plan;*
- *Morocco's geographical characteristics and natural disasters;*
- *Promotion of the issue of the participation of Moroccan veterans in the Korean War;*
- *Cooperation on aerospace industry;*
- *Bioethics-based Moroccan development strategy;*
- *The neuroscientific mechanisms of empathy and peace consciousness;*
- *Korea-Morocco collaboration in super-capacitor technology for sustainable energy;*

- *The strategic pathways for mutual growth between Morocco and Korea.*

At the outset, I would like to emphasize that the conference on Moroccan-Korean cooperation took place at the end of 2024, following 12 months of significant diplomatic events, a notable increase in economic exchanges, and enhanced cultural collaboration between the two countries. It was a year marked by several high-level visits from both sides in the political, economic, and cultural fields. Further, multiple public and private Agreements and MOUs, including three Agreements were signed by H.E. Mr. Nasser Bourita, Minister of Foreign Affairs, African Cooperation and Moroccan Expatriates, and H.E. Mr. Cho Tae-yul, Minister of Foreign Affairs of the Republic of Korea, in June, covering cooperation in the areas of climate change, social security, and the Economic Development Cooperation Fund (EDCF).

Additionally, during the Korea-Africa Summit held in June 2024, both countries signed a Joint Statement on the launch of discussions to establish a legal framework for trade and investment. This promises a strong foothold for both countries as we work towards deepening economic ties and fostering mutually beneficial growth.

The current positive relations between the two Nations are not a new development, but rather a natural progression of friendship that traced back to the 1950s, when Morocco-originated soldiers first set foot on this land as a part of the UN Battalion sent to aid the Republic of Korea during the war. From that time, our two people shared a bond as blood brothers. In his opening speech at the Korea-Africa Summit held in Seoul (June 2024), the President of the Republic of Korea acknowledged that Moroccans were among the soldiers who sacrificed their lives to defend the sovereignty of the Republic of Korea. Therefore, it was no surprise that a decade later Korea's first Embassy in Africa was opened in Morocco on July 6th, 1962, when our two countries established official diplomatic relations.

Thirteen years later, Morocco undertook a significant national initiative - The Green March- to affirm its territorial integrity and promote regional stability. In the year 1975, when Late His Majesty King Hassan II called upon Moroccan citizens, 350,000 unarmed people answered and marched into the Moroccan Sahara to peacefully assert the sovereignty and the integrity of the country. A few months later, on March 12th, 1976, the former Korean President Park, sent a letter to Late His Majesty King Hassan II, in which he said, I quote *"I am delighted to note the great victory that you have achieved through recovering the Sahara territory"*. End of quote.

Since the recovery of its Sahara, Morocco has been investing for every dollar of revenue from the region, seven dollars within a framework of solidarity. The result is plain to see: at the time of reclamation in 1975 the Human Development Indicators showed that this region lagged by 6% behind the northern areas. However, in the present day, those indicators have far exceeded the average for other regions. The Moroccan Sahara has demonstrated high levels of civic engagement, with voting participation rates exceeding the national average. Democratic processes in the region continue to be recognized by international observers, including the United Nations.

From the moment of its recovery, the Kingdom of Morocco sought ways to integrate the Moroccan Sahara issue into its national policies, landing on the broad Autonomy Initiative for the Sahara Region, presented in 2007. Significantly, this sweeping initiative qualified as 'serious and credible' by the UN Security Council and the international community, and it has proved to be not only a basis for peace, but a springboard for development. The region is becoming an economic hub, a leading center of cooperation, and a geostrategic space dedicated to stability and shared prosperity.

As you will explore in the following pages, the Moroccan Sahara issue was a central topic of discussion during the Conference on Moroccan-Korean cooperation. In this regard, I must reiterate the region's significance in Morocco's commitment to regional stability and sustainable development, fostering peace and progress in the region and in the African continent.

As a leader seeking to open the economies of the Sahel region to the Atlantic, His Majesty King Mohammed VI, May God assist Him, focused on investment in the Atlantic Coast Initiative, a Royal Vision which shifts the Moroccan southern provinces into an engine for trade and transport. Thanks to these projects, the Saharan regions -an essential link between the Atlantic, the Sahel, and sub-Saharan Africa- have also emerged as an open and attractive destination for international investment, including from the Republic of Korea.

With that in mind, I will share some important developments that the Moroccan Sahara issue underwent in 2024, under the impetus of His Majesty the King. Building from the favorable shift in position on the issue of the United States of America, Spain, and other countries during the last few years, I would like to highlight:

- The recognition of Morocco's sovereignty over its Sahara by France, a position expressed in a letter addressed by the French President and reaffirmed during his State visit to Morocco in October 2024.
- The continued international momentum in support of the Moroccan Autonomy Initiative within the European Union. Four countries have joined the other European States supporting the Moroccan initiative: Slovenia (June 2024), Finland (August 2024), Denmark (September 2024) and Estonia (November 2024). So far, 20 members of the European Union and 113 countries worldwide support the Autonomy Initiative.
- Investment opportunities provided by the southern regions of the Kingdom, demonstrated by the increasing number of countries that have opened consular representations in the region, with more than 30 consulates in Laayoune and Dakhla, representing countries from all over the world.
- The erosion of international support for the separatist entity, and the official suspension of recognition of this pseudo entity by many countries. Over the past two decades, 46 countries have withdrawn their recognition of that entity.

In the same vein, allow me to share with you the eloquent words of His Majesty the King: *"We have gained more backing for our foremost cause from the international community thanks to a better understanding of the circumstances and considerations underpinning the issue of our territorial integrity. As a result, there is growing support for our judicious autonomy initiative."*

I am confident that this book will provide readers with an accurate and objective understanding of the current political and economic situation in Moroccan Saharan Provinces, the evolution of Morocco-Korea cooperation, and the Kingdom's broader contribution to regional and African development.

In conclusion, I would like to thank Dr. John Gyun Yeol Park, President of Korea Association for Public Value, for his efforts in organizing the conference and editing this book. Further thanks go to Seoul National University of Education, particularly President Dr. Shinho Jang, and Chief of Value Ethics AI Hub Center, Dr. Hyoungbin Park.

Happy reading to all!

FORWARD

John Gyun Yeol Park
(President, Korea Association for Public Value)

There is a traditional Korean proverb, "A journey of a thousand miles begins with a single step." This proverb speaks of the importance of starting. There is also a proverb, "It is worse to give up than to not do anything." This proverb means to persevere and continue to push forward with what you have started. These proverbs can give us some lessons.

Since 2021, our Korea Association for Public Value has been holding academic conferences and publishing specialized academic journals to approach the issue of community value in an interdisciplinary manner. This book was launched to celebrate and commemorate KAPV's first collaborative initiative with the Moroccan Embassy in Seoul Korea. On December 13, 2024, KAPV hosted a major conference at Seoul National University of Education entitled: "Conference on Mutual Cooperation between Morocco and Korea: Past, Present and Future."

Recalling my private experiences, 30 years ago, I served as a United Nations peacekeeping force member in a small city called Laayoune in southern Morocco. For my private winter vacation, in 2023 winter, I visited Morocco again. Unfortunately, I was not able to revisit my previous abode. Nevertheless, during my visit, I was able to see with my own eyes how much Morocco has developed. Based on these two experiences, 30 years apart, I was able to distill my feelings into an academic paper. This became the catalyst for holding the conference once the opportunity arose to work with the Moroccan Embassy. My experiences 30 years ago have instilled in me compassion and concern for conflict zones in many parts of the world. I have also learned the importance of finding solutions to conflicts and disputes before they escalate to war. Since then, Africa has become my second home. *En réalité, depuis mon retour de la mission du PKO de NU au Maroc, l'Afrique est devenue ma deuxième maison.*

At this point, I want to recall an African proverb that says, "If you want to go fast, go alone. If you want to go far, go together." Modern civilization today tries to go too fast. We should learn from that African proverb and maintain a gradual cooperative attitude for the development of Morocco and Korea.

In particular, I would like to express my gratitude to two people. First, my gratitude is for H.E. Dr. Chafik Rachadi, Ambassador of His Majesty the King of Morocco in Seoul. He showed very high ardent patriotism for his country and devotion to making a good relationship with Republic of Korea. And he has encouraged me greatly in the development of this book. I would additionally like to express my gratitude to Professor Dr. Brendan M. Howe who is working at Ewha Womans University. Even though he was unable to attend the conference as an actual presenter at the time, he has contributed an additional chapter to enhance the quality and completeness of the book. Finally, I am very grateful to all the participants for their devotion to this book project.

April 2025

John Gyun Yeol Park

Promoting Public Value Through International Organization: Challenges and Opportunities for Regional Actors

This chapter is based on the author's article "Promoting Public Value through International Organization", *Journal of Public Value*, vol. 5, 2023): 1-10, and is reproduced here by kind permission of the Editor.

Brendan M. Howe (Ewha Womans University)

✉ bmg.howe@gmail.com

Brendan M. Howe (B.A. Hons Oxon, M.A. UKC, Ph.D. TCD) is Dean and Professor of the Graduate School of International Studies, Ewha Womans University, where he has worked since 2001. He served two terms as Associate Dean and two more as Department Chair. He currently serves as President of the *Asian Political and International Studies Association* and has been elected to serve as President of the *World International Studies Committee* from July 2025. From August 2025-August 2026 he will be supported by the *Alexander von Humboldt Foundation* for his sabbatical research at the University of Heidelberg. He has previously held research fellowships at the East-West Center in Honolulu (twice), the Freie Universität Berlin, the University of Sydney Center for International Security Studies, De La Salle University, Georgetown University, and the Korea National Defense University. Previous academic employers include the University of Dublin, Trinity College, Universiti Malaysia Sarawak, and Beijing Foreign Studies University. His research focuses on human rights, security, and development, and their intersections in the nexuses of human security, international organization, and democratic governance. He has published around 150 related books, articles, and book chapters.

I. Introduction

This chapter asks and attempts to answer the central global governance question of how can public values be generated in the international operating environment in the absence of a central governing authority? In other words, how can we govern without government? Despite competing epistemological traditions, previous research has identified an overlapping consensus on certain global public values (Howe, 2021b). These values are centered on universal wrongs which must be prevented by the international community (however it is defined) rather than universal rights. There is an overlapping cosmopolitan consensus on the need to prevent interstate war, but also on the need to prevent the most egregious crimes against vulnerable individuals and groups (Howe, 2021a). This can be interpreted as a focus on countering *summum malum* or the supreme evils of international society rather than a hope for attaining *summum bonum*, the highest or ultimate good.

Cosmopolitan public values, however, go beyond the mere rejection of wars and other atrocities. At the core, the focus is on the human security principle of freedom from the fear of imminently and arbitrarily being put to death, but also of being left to die. Yet there is also a clear overlapping consensus on the prevision for all of freedom from want of basic human needs, without which life could be dramatically foreshortened. Despite the absence of a central global government institution or leviathan (Hobbes, 1651), these global public values are promoted through a variety of formal and informal manifestations of the process of international organization. All aspects of international organization are aimed at producing some sort of public value, and the *process* of international organization has it as its central organizing theme. Multilateralism, the roles of middle powers, and both traditional and non-traditional security (NTS) cooperation are seen as key to this process. Each of these elements, however, face serious challenges in the contemporary operating environment.

The chapter, therefore, first considers the evolution of international organization and the centrality of multilateralism to the discourse. It then turns to consideration of the role of middle powers. The third analytical section addresses the shortcomings of multilateralism, especially in its universal or "maxilateral" manifestation, and the challenges faced by middle powers in achieving their global public value objectives. These realities have led to the rise of alternative "minilateral" aggregations. Yet the current minilateral manifestations are also severely limited in terms of promoting global public value, focusing solely on traditional security cooperation between great powers and bandwagoning allies. These shortcomings are addressed in the fourth analytical section. Finally, the chapter addresses the potentially important role of a new categorization of actor, second-tier powers, in generating significant international public value within certain limited parameters. Second-tier powers are the author's construct and are used to categorize those entities that have greater independent capacity for action than middle powers but are also more sensitive to cultural relativity and more focused on regional rather than universal public value creation.

II. International Organization and Multilateralism

The traditional role of the process of international organization has fundamentally, even though not exclusively, been to address the problem of interstate war (Claude, 1963, 219). Attempts to deal with this international societal scourge through a focus on shared interests and values has "given rise to major projects to construct international regimes, laws, and norms to limit war and engineer peace between polities, including states via multilateral organisations" (Richmond 2020, 14) The institutionalization of multilateral security cooperation at the global level, first under the League of Nations (albeit a false dawn), and more recently and successfully, the United Nation (UN) system, has contributed significantly to the resolution of existing conflicts and the generation of a more peaceful international society (Howe, 2021c, 502).

International organization can further be seen as a transitional process from the international anarchic conditions which generate conflict, towards the aspiration of global governance, whereby states are actively brought together to solve common problems, reconcile conflicting interests, and generate collective good, including a more peaceful and secure operating environment. Hence, international organization is the process of providing public values for the international community. Intergovernmental organizations (IOs) are representative aspects of the phase of that process which has been reached at a given time (Claude, 1963, 4).

Meanwhile, Sorpong Peou's conceptualization of international governance embraces more than the roles of formal IOs in reconciling conflicting interests and generating collective good. His conceptualization of "global public governance" offers a definition of the international system as being multilayered, polycentric, complex, and comprising formal and informal multilateral institutions, networks, regimes, and the large number of state and non-state actors required to take collective action to provide global public goods (2022, 12-13). As pointed out by Timo Kivimäki (2016), through such mechanisms, high-minded "utopian" ideals are translated into "real-world" international political action and the evaluation of these processes can be termed "constructivist pragmatism."

Multilateralism is part of this broader conceptualization, and "can be defined as the practice of co-ordinating national policies in groups of three or more states, through ad hoc arrangements or by means of institutions" and which have become increasingly important since the end of World War II (Keohane, 1990, 731). Moreover, what is distinctive about multilateralism is that the coordination of national policies of multiple states is carried out based on certain principles of ordering relations among them (Ruggie, 1992, 567). Furthermore, these should be "generalized" principles of conduct that "specify appropriate conduct for a class of actions, without regard to the particularistic interests of the parties or the strategic exigencies that may exist in any specific occurrence" (Ruggie, 1992, 571). Key elements of multilateralism include aspiration to universality, welcoming of large numbers of participants, and a strong leveling impulse (Kahler, 1992, 681). Open admission and nondiscrimination imply participation does not require the patronage of a great power, but rather is linked with the sovereign equality of states, and allows much greater participation and leverage in institutional decision-making by "states that were not great powers and could not aspire to be" (ibid.)

At the same time, institutions can be defined as "persistent and connected sets of rules, formal and informal, that prescribe behavioral roles, constrain activity, and shape expectations" of actors "which in most important cases are, need not necessarily be, states" (Keohane, 1990, 732). Such regimes are usually, but not always, accompanied by IOs "established to monitor and manage a set of rules governing state behavior in a particular issue-area" (Keohane, 1990, 733). In addition, international commissions are prominent among these new forms of collective action. They are ad hoc transnational investigative mechanisms, which can be constituted as either a temporary IO or a non-governmental organization (NGO), aimed at transforming "the assumptions and staid thinking that plague long-standing problems in international relations" (Robertson, 2020). They have featured prominently in consideration of both traditional security challenges and NTS issues of global governance and although they have been implemented at the UN since the early 1980s, they can be seen as important manifestations of the type of non-state-centric institution the influence of which has been highlighted by social constructivists in the post-Cold War operating environment.

III. The Role of Middle Powers

Middle powers have featured prominently in these international organizational initiatives to promote global values. Middle powers lack "compulsory power," the military resources to dominate others or the economic resources to bribe countries into adopting policies that they would not otherwise pursue. Yet they differ from the small or "system ineffectual" states which have little or no influence. They are, potentially, "system affecting states" which can have a significant impact within a narrower policy area, or in conjunction with others (Vom Hau, Scott, and Hulme, 2012). This also differentiates them from another class of underststudied agents, what has become known as the "rising powers," which may ultimately have the capacity to act as great powers or have already newly arrived at this level (Hameiri, Jones, and Heathershaw, 2020).

The notion of middle powers as agents of international public governance was first introduced at the end of World War II (Lee and Park, 2017). Dissatisfied with strategies dictated by great powers, countries with middling resources sought opportunities to assert their positions in the new UN system. Yet, due to ideological divides during the Cold War, proactive middlepowerism was limited for much of this period, with most of these states either bandwagoning with great powers or pursuing neutralism and nonalignment diplomacy. In 1983, however, the "Western Middle Powers and Global Poverty" project was initiated by Canada, the Netherlands, Sweden, Norway, and Denmark, as the first concrete cooperative effort among middle powers. Through the publications of the project, issues related to human rights emerged as the most instrumental subjects upon which middle powers could effectively exert their influence (Pratt, 1990).

Since then, middle powers have been identified as enthusiastic advocates of multilateral cooperation with those countries that share similar values and purposes (Lee and Park, 2017). So much so, that middle powers can be considered the chief proponents of multilateralism, with great powers preferring to focus on unilateral or bilateral mechanisms, or as addressed below, on minilateral security alliances. They have also been the initiators of most of the global international commissions.

IV. From Multilateralism to Minilateralism

In the early 1990s, freed from Cold War divides and flush from a successful collective security operation pushing Saddam Hussein's Iraq out of its occupation of Kuwait, President George H. W. Bush proclaimed a "new world order" governed according to the rule of law (Bush, 1990). His successor, William J. Clinton noted that "multilateral action held promise as never before" (New York Times, 1992). After the institutions of global governance had been placed on the back foot during the unilateralism of the George W. Bush Presidency, then Presidential candidate Barak Obama once again championed a future multilateral renaissance, and once in power "moral multilateralism" formed part of the Obama doctrine (Obama, 2007).

Unfortunately, critics have noted that optimism about such forms of multilateralism was to prove unfounded (Patrick, 2015, 115). The first administration of President Donald trump disdained multilateralism in all forms and dealt the process of global governance a blow from which it has yet to recover (Weiss, 2018, 1). The second administration is shaping up to be even more challenging. Yet, the seeds of the demise of universalism were sown well before. In a ground-breaking essay, the editor in chief of Foreign Policy, Moisés Naím, pointed to a clear pattern since the early 1990s, wherein the need for effective multi-country collaboration has soared, but at the same time multilateral talks have inevitably failed. He noted that "These failures represent not only the perpetual lack of international consensus, but also a flawed obsession with multilateralism as the panacea for all the world's ills" (Naim, 2009). Likewise, Gordan Ahl (2019) points out that although prior to the start of the 21st century, multilateral diplomacy largely took a "maxilateral" form in which institutions like the UN saw inclusivity of as many countries as possible as an end in itself, "in an increasingly divided and complicated world, this form confuses inclusivity with effectiveness as states now only sign onto vague agreements lacking legally binding force."

At the same time and in a related fashion, middle powers have experienced severe challenges in operating on the global stage, often coming up against the harsh realities of great power intransigence, but also regional epistemological resistance to their normative universalism. While many examples of multilateral avenues of global public value, including almost all international commissions, are all middle power-led, the initiators are all Western middle powers with global aspirations for their niche diplomatic endeavors. Even when attempting interregional middle power cooperation, such as in the Mexico, Indonesia, South Korea, Turkey, and Australia (MIKTA) multilateral institution, they seem doomed to fail when all that the parties had in common was self-identification as middle powers. Hence, Jeffrey Robertson (2022) has announced "the middle power moment is over."

Thus, Naim (2009) proposes that we abandon the "fool's errand" of multilateralism in favor of a new idea: "minilateralism," by which is meant "a smarter, more targeted approach, bringing to the table the smallest possible number of countries needed to have the largest possible impact on solving a particular problem." Ahl agrees, noting that "while many fear the decline or even collapse of multilateral forums, new ad-hoc coalitions of the willing provide a much-needed alternative path to efficient and strong mutual cooperation on specific issues." For Kei Koga (2022, 28), "any interstate groupings comprising only three to five members should be considered minilateral rather than multilateral." William Tow (2015, 24), agrees that minilateralism means "usually three, but sometimes four or five states meeting and interacting informally (in the absence of a governing document) to discuss issue-areas involving mutual threats to their security or, more often, to go over specific tasks related to building regional stability and order."

Security provision is the common theme among most scholars and proponents of minilateralism. Thitinan Pongsudhirak in fact identifies two emerging trends in minilateral arrangements: (1) they are no longer based on geography, and (2) they have a heavy focus on security interests (Chhangani, Tey, and Noor, 2022). Hence, current minilateralism is overwhelmingly concerned with analysis of the strategic operation of security institutions containing between three and five actors, led by the US, or on occasion, by another great power such as China.

V. Minilateral Shortcomings

The Indo-Pacific region has seen a significant rise in the number and importance of minilateral groupings. Arzan Tarapore and Brendan Taylor (2022, 2) contend that countries around the Indo-Pacific have increasingly embraced "minilateral" groupings, which they identify as "small, issue-based, informal, and uninstitutionalized partnerships—as a way of coordinating international policy action," with these groupings expanding sharply in number and ambition in the 2010s. Furthermore, rather than relying on institutions to deepen regional integration in a process inspired by European modalities, and which was their preferred option after the end of the Cold War, regional actors are "designing defense policies to dissuade potential adversaries, especially China, from revisionist behavior" (ibid.).

Early regional manifestations of the concept can be found in the Trilateral Coordination and Oversight Group (TCOG) comprising the US, Japan, and South Korea, and the Trilateral Strategic Dialogue (TSD) comprising the US, Japan, and Australia. According to Tarapore and Taylor (2022, 2), the "standard-bearer" of regional minilateralism is the Quadrilateral Security Dialogue (Quad), comprising the US, Japan, Australia, and India, which was resuscitated in 2017, while "the boldest minilateral" is AUKUS, announced in 2021, which brings together already close allies the US, Australia, and the United Kingdom (UK), to further deepen defense technology cooperation.

Yet there are major problems with the traditional security focus of Indo-Pacific minilateralism. The first problem, as argued by Koga (2022, 7), and as demonstrated particularly by the Quad and AUKUS, is that such frameworks are "largely a Western construct that attempts to fill the expectation and capability gaps in regional security systems." Given understandable regional resistance to external strategic interference, which could even be viewed as a form of neo-imperialism, they face immediate obstacles in generating public value. Indeed, there are "lingering concerns that minilateral partnerships are designed to serve large power interests and not individual state interests in the region" (Chhangani, Tey, and Noor, 2022, 3). Most suspicion must of course fall on the US, as the driving force behind the most prominent minilateral security arrangements, but there are similar concerns regarding the motivations behind Chinese minilateral initiatives (Rajagopalan, 2021, 3).

A second, related challenge to the efficacy of minilateralism, is that those that have been championed by the US, and which are the most prominent in the security field, are seen as being constructed primarily to contain a rising China, rather than to resolve regional governance issues or generate public value (Tow, 2015, 23; Anuar and Hussain, 2021, 3; Koga, 2022, 30). Competing iterations of minilateralism risk narrowing the space available for small and middle powers, and even second-tier powers to operate as they are thrust into "with us or against us" narratives (Job, 2020, 2; Boon and Teo, 2022, 60). Forcing regional actors to choose undermines the coherence of the minilateral organization, as participants will demonstrate different degrees of commitment (Rajagopalan, 2021, 7; Chhangani, Tey, and Noor, 2022, 2-3). In fact, most other actors would rather not choose sides between great powers but would rather maintain a degree of "strategic ambiguity" (Boon and Teo, 2022, 60).

This links to a third problematic area for regional security multilateralism, that of its exclusionary rather than inclusive nature. To contribute meaningfully toward regional order-building and public value generation, minilateral initiatives need to generate support from regional constituencies (Koga, 2022, 30). Yet Patrick has noted (2015, 117 & 130) that such institutions threaten to "replace the provision of international public goods with club goods benefiting a narrower range of countries, while marginalizing formal international institutions," and "unless used deftly and judiciously, minilateralism risks undermining the legitimacy and effectiveness of indispensable international organizations and even accelerating the world's coalescence into rival coalitions."

In the Middle East and Maghreb, the challenges to multilateralism, both global and regional, have proven insurmountable. The region has evolved into an arena for great power contestation and proxy warfare, much to the detriment of the human security of those who live there. In response, in this region in particular, "minilateralism has gained popularity, as many countries grapple with the repercussions of decades of conflict, instability, and foreign intervention" (Mladenov, 2023). These initiatives include the India, France, UAE trilateral defense, energy, and technology cooperation, Negev Forum, which brings together the US, Israel, the UAE, Egypt, Morocco, and Bahrain, and the 2021 "Partnership for the Future" (the I2U2 format) between the US, India, Israel, and the UAE (ibid.).

Even more so than the Asia-Pacific, however, the "minilateral moment" in the region is in danger of being seen as an opportunity for great powers like the US (but also China, Russia, and in this case India) to pursue their traditional security agendas (Samaan, 2023). Here, then, we return to the inherently less confrontational nature of NTS issues and policy prescription for regional actors.

VI. Disruptive Innovation and Second—Tier Actors

In 2005, United Nations (UN) Secretary-General Kofi Annan referenced the interrelatedness of the three pillars of the UN by noting, "[W]e will not enjoy security without development, development without security, and neither without respect for human rights. Unless all these causes are advanced, none will succeed" (Annan, 2005). In doing so he neatly encapsulated the progress made by the evolution of security and governance conceptualizations, as well as ongoing challenges. Over time, security provision in both theory and practice, has become increasingly entwined with other global value aspirations and provisions. Policy prescription and obligations for those who govern, as well as putative peacebuilders, therefore, must increasingly consider spillover between these diverse agendas, and this has been reflected in the newly emerging humanitarian-development-peace nexus (HDPN) discourse (Howe, 2022).

As discussed above, there remain operational shortcomings at the global governance level, more than a decade and a half after Annan's original call to action for a more integrated and human-centered approach to peace and security. Yet these amount to "noble opportunities" for a new category of actor. Second-tier actors are herein conceptualized as actors that have greater than "middling" power resources, but also concentrate their resources into geographically distinct regions. They are therefore distinguished from traditional middle powers with their more limited resources, but global normative aspirations. They are also distinct from rising powers, as they do not have great power aspirations. In the Indo-Pacific, key candidates for second-tier activism include South Korea, Japan, and Indonesia. In the Middle East and the Maghreb, they are Morocco, Turkey, and Saudi Arabia (Murciano, 2025).

What then can and should the regional second-tier powers and their societies do to promote solutions to international public value challenges? First, rather than lament geostrategic inadequacies and challenges, it would benefit regional second-tier actors to divert at least some of their resources to cooperation to generate public value in ways that are not dependent on global consensus, or the involvement or acquiescence of the great powers. In business theory, the term "disruptive innovation" was coined to describe an innovation that creates a new market and value network and eventually disrupts an existing market and value network (Christensen, 1997). Lingfei Wu, Dashun Wang, and James Evans (2019) later generalized this term to identify disruptive science and technological advances. Basically, it means coming up with radically different policies and ways of doing things that challenge and unsettle existing norms, in the hope of achieving progress. Here it is proposed that we adopt the term to apply to the radical out of the box thinking and practices needed to address both traditional security and NTS challenges in the regional context.

These would include but would not be limited to minilateral NTS cooperation between three to five second tier powers, and regional, as opposed to global, international commissions. Such commissions could be launched on such varied issues as NTS challenges like regional pandemic response, transnational pollution, regional refugee flows, and disaster risk reduction traditional security issues such as nuclear proliferation, and governance failure, and those issues which bridge two challenges, such as resource and water security. There are numerous advantages to taking this type of institutional approach. First, it would empower new second-tier agents. Second, it would remove the great power tensions from NTS security promotion. Third, it would allow for spillover from NTS problem solving to traditional security de-escalation and confidence building by establishing a non-threatening, non-confrontational cooperative culture of responsiveness in the region being addressed.

As new actors, second-tier powers have a golden opportunity to pursue their own interests while simultaneously promoting an expansion of the international provision of public value and public goods. They, therefore, have a "responsibility to disrupt" in addition to the global public duty of the responsibility to protect. The new market envisioned here is the expansion of public value provision through international organization to include greater, and more targeted NTS cooperation. As such it fundamentally critiques and disrupts the old ways of doing things.

■ References

Ahl, G. "The Benefits of Minilateral Diplomacy," *Lighthouse Journal*, University of Oxford, April 18, 2019. https://www.lighthousejournal.co.uk/post/the-benefits-of-minilateral-diplomacy

Anuar, A., and Hussain, N. "Challenges to Minilateralism" in *Minilateralism for Multilateralism in the Post-COVID Age* (pp. 3-5). S. Rajaratnam School of International Studies. https://www.jstor.org/action/doBasicSearch?si=1&Query=au:%22Amalina+Anuar%22

Boon, H. and Teo, S. (2022), "Caught in the Middle? Middle Powers amid U.S.-China Competition." *Asia Policy* 17(4): 59-76. DOI Address https://doi.org/10.1353/asp.2022.0058

Bush, G.H.W. "Out of these troubled times··· a New World Order." Text of the President's speech to a joint session of Congress. Washington Post, September 12, 1990. https://www.washingtonpost.com/archive/politics/1990/09/12/bush-out-of-these-troubled-times-a-new-world-order/b93b5cf1-e389-4e6a-84b0-85f71bf4c946/

Chhangani, A., Tey, A., and Noor, E. "Is Minilateralism the Future of the Indo-Pacific."

Asia Society Summary Report. March 29, 2022. https://asiasociety.org/sites/default/files/2022-04/ASPI_IndoPacific_SummReport_finalize.pdf

Christensen, C. The Innovator's Dilemma: When New Technologies Cause Great Firms to Fail (Boston: Harvard Business School Press). 1997.

Claude, I. Swords Into Plowshares: The Problems and Progress of International Organization. (New York: Random House). 1963.

Hameiri, S., Jones, L., and Hethershaw, J. Rising Powers and State Transformation. (Abingdon: Routledge). 2020.

Hobbes, T. Leviathan, or The Matter, Forme and Power of a Common Wealth Ecclesiasticall and Civil. (Oxford: Clarendon Press). 1651 [1909].

Howe, B. (2021a), "Public Value and Human Security." *Journal of Public Value*, 1(1): 13–22. DOI address https://doi.org/10.53581/jopv.2021.1.1.13

Howe, B. 'Non-traditional security leadership and cooperation in the face of great power conflict: The rise of new actors' *Asian Journal of Peacebuilding* 10(1): 243–270 (2022). DOI address https://doi.org/10.18588/202202.00a211

Howe, B. "Challenges to and Opportunities for International Organisation in East Asia' *Global Society* 35(4): 501–521 (2021c). DOI address https://doi.org/10.1080/13600826.2021.1942800

Howe, B. "Universal Public Values and Regional Divergence." *Journal of Public Value* 2(1): 1–14 (2021b). DOI address https://doi.org/10.53581/jopv.2021.2.1.1

Job, B. "Between a Rock and a Hard Place: The Dilemmas of Middle Powers," *Issues and Studies* 56(2): 1–24. (2020). DOI address https://doi.org/10.1142/S1013251120400081

Kahler, M. "Multilateralism with Small and Large Numbers" *International Organization* 46(3): 681–708. (1992). DOI address https://www.jstor.org/stable/2706992

Keohane, R. "Multilateralism: An Agenda for Research" *International Journal* 45(4): 731–764. (1990). DOI address https://doi.org/10.2307/40202705

Kivimäki, T. Paradigms of Peace. (London: Imperial College Press). 2016.

Kofi Annan, "In Larger Freedom: Towards Development, Security and Human Rights for All", *Report of the Secretary-General*, A/59/2005, 21 March 2005, https://www.un.org/en/events/pastevents/in_larger_freedom.shtml

Koga, K. "A New Strategic Minilateralism in the Asia-Pacific." *Asia Policy* 17(4): 27-34 (2022).

Lee, S. and Park, C. "Korea's Middle Power Diplomacy for Human Security: A Global and Regional Approach" *Journal of International and Area Studies* 24(1): 21-44. (2017). DOI address http://doi.org/10.23071/jias.2017.24.1.21

Mladenov, N. "Minilateralism: A Concept That is Changing the World Order." *Washington Institute Policy Analysis* April 14, 2023. https://www.washingtoninstitute.org/policy-analysis/minilateralism-concept-changing-world-order

Murciano, G. "Unpacking the Geopolitics of Three Theatres: A perspective from the Middle East" *Geopolitics and International Order*. Friedrich Ebert Stiftung. January 22, 2025. https://asia.fes.de/news/middle-east-and-the-three-theatres.html?fbclid=IwY2xjawIGySNleHRuA2FlbQIxMQABHac0REAji WaI1ZlmSm5l1knJqeMs1ZTXvZM4e3oaHtQJb2eZaskOMoDkeg_aem_ ACczuO9lzfWL_053vtGdbQ

Naim, M. "Minilateralism: The Magic Number to Get Real International Action". *Foreign Policy*, June 21, 2009. http://foreignpolicy.com/2009/06/21/minilateralism/

New York Times. "The 1992 Campaign: Excerpts from Clinton's Speech on Foreign Policy Leadership." August 14. https://www.nytimes.com/1992/08/14/us/the-1992-campaign-excerpts-from-clinton-s-speech-on-foreign-policy-leadership.html

Obama, B. "Remarks of Senator Barack Obama to the Chicago Council on Global Affairs", April 23, 2007. http://www.cfr.org/elections/remarks-senator-barackobama-chicago-council-global-affairs/p13172

Patrick, S. "The New 'New Multilateralism': Minilateral Cooperation, but at What Cost?" *Global Summitry* 1(2): 115-134. (2015). DOI address https://doi.org/10.1093/global/guv008

Peou, S. Global Public Governance: Toward World Government? (Singapore: World Scientific Publishing). 2022.

Pratt, C. Middle power internationalism: The North-South dimension. (Montreal: McGill-Queen's University Press). 1990.

Rajagopalan, R. "Explaining the Rise of Minilaterals in the Indo-Pacific." *ORF Issue Brief No. 490*, September 2021, Observer Research Foundation. https://www.orfonline.org/research/explaining-the-rise-of-minilaterals-in-the-indo-pacific/

Rawls, J. "The Idea of an Overlapping Consensus" *Oxford Journal of Legal Studies* 7(1): 1-25. (1987). DOI address https://doi.org/10.1093/ojls/7.1.1

Richmond, O. Peace in International Relations (2E). (Abingdon: Routledge). 2020.

Robertson, J. "In Search of a Middle-power Rethink on North Korea Policy." *The Interpreter*, November 25, 2020. https://www.lowyinstitute.org/the-interpreter/searchmiddle-power-rethink-north-korea-policy?fbclid=IwAR1Uz2RfQNO4rNqrsFetFnuJ6mlwMJ8XqY_KfbbCXMcX01AjQ1HIWMo4RXE

Robertson, J. "MIKTA: The Middle Power's Last Hurrah?" *Global Governance*, December 28, 2022. https://gjia.georgetown.edu/2022/12/28/mikta-the-middle-powers-last-hurrah/

Ruggie, J. "Multilateralism: the Anatomy of an Institution" *International Organization* 46(3): 561-598. (1992). DOI address https://doi.org/10.1017/S0020818300027831

Samaan, J.-L. *The Minilateral Moment in the Middle East: An Opportunity for US Regional Policy? Atlantic Council Issue Brief* (2023). http://www.jstor.org/stable/resrep51796

Tarapore, A. and Taylor, B. "Minilaterals and Deterrence: A Critical New Nexus." *Asia*

Policy 17(4): 2–7. DOI address https://doi.org/10.1353/asp.2022.0068

Tow, W. "The Trilateral Strategic Dialogue, Minilateralism, and Asia-Pacific Order Building." Stimson Center April 1, 2015 https://www.jstor.org/stable/resrep11008.7

Vom Hau, M., Scott, J., and Hulme, D. "Beyond the BRICs: Alternative Strategies of Influence in the Global Politics of Development." European Journal of Development Research 24 (2): 187–204. (2012). DOI address https://doi.org/10.1057/ejdr.2012.6

Weiss, T. "The UN and Multilateralism under Siege in the 'Age of Trump.'" *Global Summitry* 4(1): 115–134. (2018). DOI address https://doi.org/10.1093/global/guy013

Wu, L., Wang, D., & Evans, J. "Large teams develop and small teams disrupt science and technology" *Nature* 566 (2019): 378–382. DOI address https://doi.org/10.1038/s41586-019-0941-9

Chapter 2

———

Sustainable Land Redevelopment Strategy of Morocco based on an Eco Ethics Perspective

This chapter is based on the article: Gyun Yeol Park, Jungbae Bang, Hojong Lee, Daechol Kwon, Jongnam Choi, "Sustainable Land Redevelopment Strategy of Morocco Based on an Eco Ethics Perspective", *Studies on Humanities and Social Sciences*, 6(1), 2023): 1-10, and is reproduced here by kind permission of the Editor.

John Gyun Yeol Park (Gyeongsang National University)

✉ pgy556@gnu.kr

John Gyun Yeol Park is a professor in the Department of Ethics Education at Gyeongsang National University (GNU), Jinju, Republic of Korea. He has taught political philosophy or political ethics, such as North Korean Studies, International Affairs and Ethics, and National Security since 2007. Before joining GNU, he was a research fellow at the Korea National Defense University. He is the author of several books, including Community, Ethics and Security on the Korean Peninsula (Co-written in English), National Security and Moral Education (in Korean), Peace Security and Moral Education (in Korean), National Security and Military Ethics (in Korean), and others. His current research interests are political ethics and its evaluation. Now he is a president for Korea Association for Public Value which has published Journal of Public Value since June 2021.

I. Introduction

Human beings are born with the freedom to pursue self-actualization without obstacles or constraints (Berlin, 1969). However, many countries in Africa do not enjoy this basic freedom due to the harsh natural environment and colonial exploitation by Western powers in the past. In particular, the vast Sahara Desert, located in the north-central part of Africa, appears to symbolize the poor economic and environmental situations of many African countries. In order to halt the rapid progression of desertification in the region and improve the quality of life of its inhabitants by expanding green spaces, systematic national spatial development planning is required. However, according to the United Nations Environment Program (UNEP), population growth, deforestation, cropland expansion, overgrazing, drought, lack of precipitation, and inadequate development planning have rendered much of the Sahel barren in the 20th century (Kandji, 2006). In 2007, the African Union (AU) launched the Pan-African Great Green Wall (GGW) initiative to combat desertification of the Sahara and Sahel region on a multinational scale. This multinational project aims to prevent desertification and curb the expansion of deserts by creating a 15 km wide and 7,775 km long green belt stretching from Dakar, Senegal, to Djibouti on the Red Sea by 2030 (Dok & Berlinger, 2022). However, this project is estimated to have achieved only 4-20% of its planned goals (Henderson, 2022).

It is difficult enough to achieve development projects for a country. However, it is even more challenging to succeed in a project like GGW that involves more than 20 countries. Thus, for multinational development initiatives such as the GGW project in Africa to be successful, it is recommended to support the development plans of particular countries with great development potential to create successful cases of national development projects and then gradually spread these successful cases to neighboring countries. This study focuses on the sustainable land development of Morocco among the countries with the Sahara desert in their territories. Morocco's geographical proximity to developed countries in Europe and North America makes it easier to get technical and financial support to overcome the current economic and environmental situations. In addition, although Morocco is not a participant in the GGW Project, its experience in successful land development plans can be a convincing case for replicating its successes and scaling up its achievements eastward across the Sahara.

This study considers the countries of the northern Sahel region bordering the Sahara Desert. However, it focuses on Morocco, examining its climatic and topographical characteristics and proposing actionable measures to rebuild the country. In particular, many countries in the sub-Saharan region have not yet achieved the status of developed nations despite being relatively well endowed with water resources and being heavily forested. This study focuses on the role of good citizenship to analyze the causes that led to this situation using an interdisciplinary approach.

Thus, this study provides a comprehensive roadmap for the Moroccan people to aspire to and realize a genuine positive peace (Galtung, 1996) beyond the mere restoration of their forests. However, this study may be less theoretically rigorous because it adopts a variety of approaches simultaneously, ranging from normative requests to budgeting and civic education.

II. Theoretical Background

1. Theoretical Background

Land development requires a diverse theoretical background. Traditional approaches to land development mainly focus on utilitarian efficiency. However, an eco ethical perspective that views the land as an important partner to humans rather than an object to be overcome and exploited has important implications. There are diverse eco ethical theories.

First, Schweitzer's reverence for life: an apocryphal view of life. Schweitzer points out that advances in science and technology and the industrial society that accompanied them under the influence of a modern scientific perspective led to an understanding of nature as value-neutral and governed by mechanical laws. Instead, he believed that all life has intrinsic value and, thus, deserves our reverence and that life is inherently good and worthy of respect. Accordingly, he highlighted that a morally good person has an attitude of awe and respect for the inherent value of each life (Goodin, 2007).

Second, Taylor's vitalism: Taylor explains that the claim that every living thing has its goodness is meaningful because every living thing is the "teleological center of life." He understood that each species has unique properties that determine particular goods for that species, such as growth, development, and reproduction, which are given to being itself with the will to live. From this perspective, he believed that humans are members of the Earth's community of life in the same sense and conditions as other living things and that all species, including humans, are part of an interdependent system. He also believed that every living thing pursues its goodness in its own way and that humans are not considered inherently superior to other living things (Taylor, 2020[1985]).

Third, Habermas's Theory of Communicative Action: Strictly speaking, this theory cannot be considered an eco ethical theory.

However, this theory is necessary to discuss the procedural problems of the "Four Major Rivers Restoration Project" in South Korea. Habermas emphasized public discussion and communication as important democratic principles. The theory argues that democracy should be implemented through public discussion and communication and explains that it is important to promote consensus and fair decision-making among citizens. He believes that democratic systems can be more firmly grounded through this process. He also argued that public spaces of discussion and communication, called the public spheres, are essential to democracy. In these public spheres, citizens should be able to participate in political decision-making by freely sharing their opinions and debating public issues. Habermas emphasizes the importance of deliberation and communication in democracy, arguing that political decisions should be made through public debate and consensus among citizens. While his theory emphasizes the importance of public debate and deliberation in the workings of democracy, it also emphasizes that policy decisions should not be rushed through without a clear sense of great cause (Habermas, 1962, 1984).

Fourth, Modest Anthropocentrism: It can be conceptually confused with the latter in the traditional strong anthropocentrism framework. Modest anthropocentrism is the position that we are anthropocentric because we are humans. The word "modest" refers to the position that we cannot say we have dignity above the entire ecological environment just because we are humans.

2. Approaches

Just as there are various theories of eco ethics about the land, so are the approaches to land. First, the conservationist approach to the natural environment: This approach is based on the approach of Gifford Pinchot, an American forester and early ecological environmentalist. This conservationism is often referred to as conservation management. This conservationism states that nature should be left undisturbed as a treasure trove of resources in terms of their utility value in enabling the development of human civilization and the enrichment of human life. However, this conservationism also holds that nature can be managed and protected and used wisely to benefit the long-term well-being of humans. Pinchot supported a plan to build a reservoir in the glacial Hetch Hetchy Valley, northwest of Yosemite National Park, to address a severe water shortage in San Francisco in the early 20th century. He did so because he understood that even highly protected natural resources could be used effectively to meet desperate human needs (Pinchot, 1910, 1914; Hays, 1959).

Second, the social justice approach to the environment: This approach emphasizes an approach from theories of justice to environmental issues, in which environmental justice is not only about content justice but also about procedural justice, which emphasizes participation in the decision-making and implementation of environmental initiatives. From this perspective, the debate based on democratic processes should be conducted not only in the decision-making processes related to the development of nature but also in implementation processes to restore it (Bell & Carrick, 2017; Gellers & Jeffords, 2018).

Third, the modern ecological approach to the environment based on a dynamic understanding of nature: This ecocentric approach is consistent with an ecological awareness that emphasizes ecosystems. However, this approach does not focus on the homeostasis of the ecosystems but is based on coherent philosophical ethics consistent with the ecological awareness that change is normal. This approach requires a sufficient explanation of the relationship between the parts and the whole of nature and the dynamics of change that govern nature as a whole. Similarly, a certain level of explanation is required to change a phenomenon to return nature to its "original" state (Botkin, 1990).

Fourth, sustainability. If land development is promoted in a way that destroys the environment, it will cause further damage to humans in the long run. It is an unsustainable development. Sustainable development focuses on developing land without harming the environment. In this context, the United Nations created 17 Sustainable Development Goals (SDGs), a blueprint for achieving a better and more sustainable future for all. The 17 SDFs are no poverty, zero hunger, good health and well-being, quality education, gender equality, clean water and sanitation, affordable and clean energy, decent work and economic growth, industry, innovation and infrastructure, reduced inequality, sustainable cities and communities, responsible consumption and production, climate action, life below water, life on land, peace, justice and strong institutions, and partnerships. Of the 17 goals, five are related to the environment, demonstrating that sustainable economic development must go hand in hand with environmental conservation.

III. Natural and Human Environment of Morocco

1. Topography and Climate

Morocco has diverse topography, including the Rif Mountains in the north, the Atlas Mountains in the center, plateaus in the east, plains and coast in the west, and desert in the south (Figure 1). A large part of Morocco is mountainous. The Atlas Mountains run through the center of Morocco, forming a natural divide between the Mediterranean northern coastal zone and the southern interior regions, which lie on the edge of the Sahara Desert.

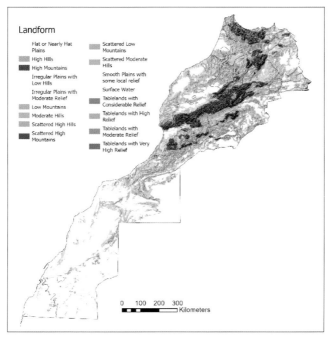

Landform

Flat or Nearly Flat Plains
High Hills
High Mountains
Irregular Plains with Low Hills
Irregular Plains with Moderate Relief
Low Mountains
Moderate Hills
Scattered High Hills
Scattered High Mountains

Scattered Low Mountains
Scattered Moderate Hills
Smooth Plains with some local relief
Surface Water
Tablelands with Considerable Relief
Tablelands with High Relief
Tablelands with Moderate Relief
Tablelands with Very High Relief

0   100   200   300
Kilometers

Figure 1_A topographic map of Morocco showing landforms in different colors
Source: World Ecological Facets Landform Classes

The High Atlas Mountains lies in central Morocco. It rises west at the Atlantic coast and stretches to the Moroccan-Algerian border to the east. At the Atlantic and to the southwest, the elevation of the mountain range falls steeply. It transitions to the coast and the Anti-Atlas range. To the north, the range descends less abruptly. The Anti-Atlas extends from the Atlantic Ocean southwest of Morocco toward the northeast. It borders the Sahara in the south. The Middle Atlas is the northernmost of the three Atlas ranges. The Middle Atlas lies north of the High Atlas, separated by the Moulouya and Oum Er-Rbia rivers, and south of the Rif mountains, separated by the Sebou River. The Middle Atlas also experiences more rain than the ranges to the south, making it an important water catchment for the coastal plains. To the west of the Middle Atlas are the main coastal plains of Morocco, with many of the major cities.

Morocco's climate varies with its diverse topography and the effects of the cold ocean current, Canary Current, off the Atlantic coast. Morocco's climatic regions extend from the Mediterranean climate in the northern coastal zone, temperate and alpine climate in the central mountainous regions, to desert climate in the southern interior regions (Figure 2).

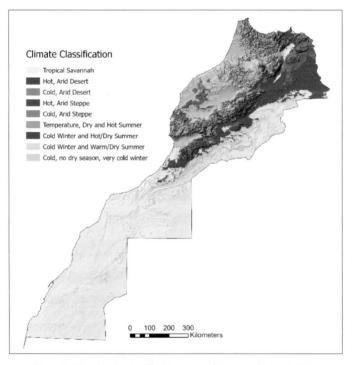

Figure 2_The climate classification map of Morocco for 1991-2020

Source: Koppen-Geiger Climate Classification

Typical Mediterranean climate dominates the coastal Mediterranean regions and some parts of the Atlantic coast. The cooler sea breezes consistently blow over the coastal regions, which helps to get more moderated temperatures, especially at the height of the summertime. Summers are hot to moderately hot and dry, with daily average highs around 30°C. Winters are mild and wet, with daily average temperatures around 10°C. Annual Precipitation varies from 600 to 800 mm in the west to 350-500 mm in the east (Figure 3). The coastal lowlands in the northwest have moderate temperatures, even in summer (Figure 4). Approximately 95% of the population lives in this climate region.

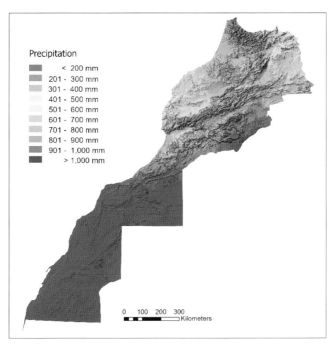

Figure 3_Annual mean precipitation of Morocco for 2000-2022

Source: WorldClim Global Mean Precipitation

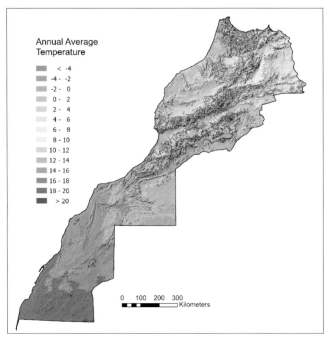

Figure 4_Annual average temperature of Morocco for 1981-2010

Source: ArcGIS Living Atlas

A wet temperate climate zone with moderate precipitation is located on the northwest side of the Middle and High Atlas Mountains, facing westerly. Winters are cold, and temperatures fall below the freezing point. Annual precipitation varies between 500 and 900 mm. On the contrary, the rain shadow effect leads to a dry climate with long and hot summers in the southeast, leeward slopes of the Atlas Mountains. Rainfall is limited, and annual precipitation is between 200 and 350 mm. Alpine climate zones are found at higher elevations in the Atlas Mountains.

Arid and desert climates with extreme heat and very low moisture prevail in the lowland regions east of the Atlas range of the southeastern most portion of Morocco near the Algerian borders through most of the year. A hot, dry wind that originates from the vast deserts in the southeast and blows in the spring or early summer. It brings daytime temperatures of over 40°C, and the relative humidity can drop to 5% or even less. However, temperatures can drop dramatically at night, especially in December and January.

2. Two Ecological Regions with Different Natural and Human Environments

Morocco has various ecological regions, from Mediterranean forests through alpine forests to the north Saharan steppe, because of its diverse topography and climates. Figure 5 shows that the northern and southern parts of Morocco, bordered by the Atlas Mountains, have distinctly different ecological regions.

2.1. North of the Atlas Mountains

Many forests in the north of the Atlas Mountains are under many threats. Deforestation has long been an environmental issue. Many hilly areas have been cleared for farming. Isolated patches of the Mediterranean conifer and mixed forests appear at mid to high elevations in the Rif Mountains, Middle Atlas, and High Atlas Mountains, where average yearly rainfall reaches 1,000 mm. Thick and lush forests are widely distributed in the valleys. The endemic Atlas cedar dominates the forest's canopy, and other tree species, including oak, conifer, yew, firs, and juniper, cover the forest's understory. Deforestation is the major threat to this forest. Many conservational measures have been established to conserve these forests. The Mediterranean woodlands and forests cover the Mediterranean coastal plain, rugged hills, and the slopes of the Atlas Mountains. Dominating temperate tree species include the Aleppo pine, holm oaks, junipers, Atlantic fir, and cork oak. The Mediterranean dry woodlands and steppe, covering inland plateaus and the High Atlas mountain ranges, provide habitats for many grazing animals.

Water scarcity is an ongoing problem. The coastal plain is the backbone of the country's agriculture. Most arable land, comprising 18% of the country, is located in the coastal plain region. Agriculture accounts for 88% of water consumption in Morocco (The Water Diplomat, 2022), mostly for growing water-intensive crops and mostly intended for export, such as watermelon, avocado, almonds, and citrus fruit, at the expense of local subsistence farming.

In agricultural lands with a lack of rainfall, irrigation supports agricultural activities. Groundwater has also been overexploited for agricultural purposes. Farmers usually live on the hillside, not near their fields, similar to those in southern Spain. This residential pattern further destroys the existing forests.

An increase in demography, along with agricultural intensification, has led to a significant increase in water consumption (Molle and Tanouti,

2017) and worsened water scarcity in Morocco. As shown in Figure 6, the highest population density is found along the Atlantic and Mediterranean coasts, home to some of Morocco's largest cities, including Rabat and Casablanca. Several densely populated agglomerations are also found scattered through the Atlas Mountains.

2.2. South of the Atlas Mountains

In the south of the Atlas Mountains, small patches of trees are usually distributed in the riparian environment. The North Saharan steppe and woodlands cover the western and northern border of the larger Sahara Desert, experiencing rainfall ranging between 50 to 100 mm during the cooler winter and maximum temperatures reaching 45°C. This vegetation is greatly threatened by overgrazing and water pollution in the riparian habitats.

Agricultural monocultures, mining companies, and, recently, solar power plants consume the most water in this region. Due to the overconsumption and lack of precipitation, water from the valleys around Ouarzazate in the al-Mansour Eddahbi dam is currently below its capacity. Much like the north of the Atlas Mountains, large volumes of water are used not to grow locally adapted and resilient species but to cultivate water-intensive commercial crops, such as watermelon and citrus fruit. For example, large-scale investments in watermelon production in Skoura, a city in southern Ouarzazate, seriously jeopardize local water resources for local subsistence farming.

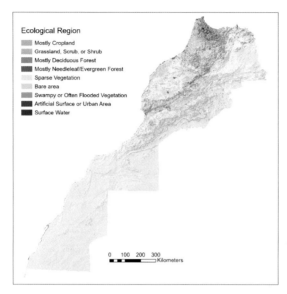

Ecological Region

■ Mostly Cropland
■ Grassland, Scrub, or Shrub
■ Mostly Deciduous Forest
■ Mostly Needleleaf/Evergreen Forest
□ Sparse Vegetation
□ Bare area
■ Swampy or Often Flooded Vegetation
■ Artificial Surface or Urban Area
■ Surface Water

0   100 200 300
Kilometers

Figure 5_Ecological regions in Morocco

Source: European Space Agency Climate Change Initiative-Land Cover (2018)

Population (100 m)

■ 980
3,44721e-05

0   100 200 300
Kilometers

Figure 6_Population Distribution in Morocco

Source: WorldPop (2020)

This region does not receive adequate precipitation for agriculture due to climatic factors (Figure 5, 6). As a result, there is limited grazing on the foothills of the High Atlas Mountains and sparse grazing on the open desert. Few forests and very limited arable land make it unsuitable for human settlements. However, the underlying reason for the region's water scarcity is the poor management of the water resources provided by the ice caps and the two mountain lakes located in the foothills of the High Atlas Mountains. Along with further significant water losses in water distribution networks, the rivers downstream have dried up and become wadis. In order to achieve sustainable development for the region, efficient catchment of water resources must be implemented, and crops must be selected to suit the climatic conditions.

IV. Direction to the Sustainable National Land Development in Morocco

1. Evaluating Past Cases

1.1. The Great Green Wall for the Sahara and Sahel Initiative

Under the Sahara and Sahel Initiative (SSI) project, the massive Green Great Wall of Africa project involves more than 20 African countries, including Ethiopia and Senegal, to combat the desertification of the Sahara Desert. However, the future of this project is not optimistic because of the following reasons.

First and foremost, this project is unsustainable because it uses groundwater to build greenery. The financial support for the project has been unfulfilled. The tree-planting project has been carried out in the absence of resources to replace the demand for wood for shelter and firewood for cooking. As a result, it has created an even greater tree deficit in the local communities. The restoration of the Sahara Desert is impossible without self-sustaining forests that can hold water for long periods and support non-human life.

1.2. The Water Highway Project in Morocco

Vizy and Cook (2012) predicted that the northern part of Africa is more likely to suffer from an increase in temperature and a decrease in the amount and frequency of precipitation due to the recent climate change. Like other countries in North Africa, climate change trends have already put great pressure on Morocco on multiple dimensions, affecting the resilience of forest ecosystems and the agriculture sector, particularly due to water scarcity. According to the ND-GAIN Index (Notre Dame Global Adaptation Initiative, 2023), Morocco is recognized as vulnerable to climate change impacts due to its combination of geographic and social factors. According to a World Bank press release on July 20, 2022, Morocco is among the world's most water-stressed countries (World Bank, 2022).

The hydrology of Morocco is characterized by great spatial variation: a sharp gradient in annual precipitation decreasing from the north to the south due to its diverse topography and the effects of the cold ocean current off the Atlantic coast. In order to alleviate the water stress in the south of the High Atlas Mountains, the Water Highway project has been proposed to redistribute the available water (annually 860×106 m3) from the wet north to the arid southern regions (Figure 7).

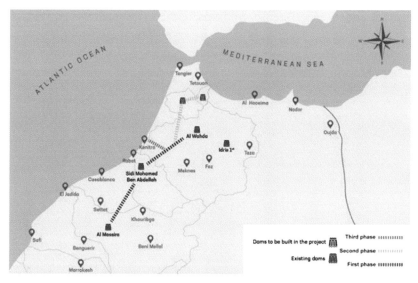

Figure 7_The Water Highway Project in Morocco
Source: Moçayd et al., 2020

However, despite its great potential positive impacts, the success of the project largely depends on the amount of water that will be available in the future. Moçayd et al. (2020) stated that the Water Highway project needs to be carried out carefully and implemented in a phased manner due to the uncertainties in the future precipitation introduced by climate change.

2. Direction of National Development Considering Morocco's Geographical Features

A comprehensive approach to environmental and sustainable development must be implemented to prevent desertification and land degradation and to achieve efficient land development (Bellefontaine, 2011). If the focus is solely on land development, the environment will be degraded, and, as a result, sustainable development cannot be achieved. Conversely, if the focus is solely on environmental management, the country's economic growth will stagnate, and the local residents' survival will be threatened, ultimately leading to the failure of sustainable land development efforts. Thus, environment management and economic development must be properly balanced to achieve long-term sustainable land development. A water management system to prevent waste and loss of water and utilize it efficiently, an environmental protection system to prevent forest degradation and increase green spaces, and a resident support and education system to compensate residents for displacement and losses due to environmental protection should be comprehensively implemented. In this context, this study proposes several directions for sustainable, efficient land development that take into account the geography and topography of Morocco, including the following.

2.1. Building Water Storage Capacity: Maintenance of the Self-Sustainability of Mountain Lakes and an Eco-Friendly Method to Trap Water using Bamboo

The High Atlas Mountains, which runs through the center of the country, is the most important source of water for Morocco, which has an arid to semi-arid climate. Due to the altitude of the High Atlas Mountains, precipitation falls in the form of rain and snow. In some areas, annual precipitation exceeds 800 mm, with a significant portion of the precipitation falling as snow (Hanich, 2022). Snowmelt is used for a variety of purposes. However, it is particularly important for irrigation, which accounts for more than 85% of the water available to Morocco. Therefore, this mountain range can be considered Morocco's "water tower," supplying fresh water to the vast arid plains downstream (Khabb et al., 2013). Nevertheless, Morocco faces increasing pressure on its water resources due to climate change, decreasing precipitation, increasing drought frequency, population growth, and urbanization. The current water resource use pattern and water withdrawal method do not allow the sustainable use of water resources. Therefore, securing an uninterrupted water supply for the sustainable socioeconomic development of the country has been a constant concern for Morocco, a water-stressed country (CESE, 2014).

One way to address this problem is to build water storage capacity. Various construction methods should be implemented, which can trap rainwater or snowmelt flowing down from the Atlas Mountains so that the water is not wasted and can control its gradual release of stored water. Among them, the Water Storage and Supply Control Device using Bamboo would be one of the good alternatives to trap rainwater or snowmelt (Figure 9). This device was invented by Gyun Yeol Park, one of the authors of this paper. The utility model was submitted to the Korean Intellectual Property Office (Park, 2023).

This eco-friendly device contains a water storage and supply regulation device using bamboo that effectively stores surface water and slowly releases it by forming multiple underground walls. This device connects multiple rainwater storage units in a belt and plants them around trees, keeping plants hydrated for longer periods. The device also allows for the vertical movement of rainwater by interconnecting multiple storage units. The water outlet at the bottom is designed to have a smaller inner diameter than the openings between the storage compartments, so the rainwater stored inside gradually drains into the ground through the narrow outlet (Figure 9a). The discharged rainwater spreads out while wetting the soil and continuously moisturizing the roots of the plants. Mounting multiple units will allow plants to grow even during droughts. The device can further be equipped with a storage container made of a material that can hold rainwater at the bottom of the tree. In summary, this device is made of bamboo, which can be easily obtained locally. It has the great advantage of effectively storing rainwater and supplying it over a long period. Additionally, the parts that store and deliver water in this device are made of eco-friendly materials. Therefore, even if the device is left unattended for a long time, it will decompose on its own, preventing environmental pollution (Figure 10).

Figure 9_The Water Storage and Supply Control Device using Bamboo: an eco-friendly method to trap water using bamboo (Park, 2023)

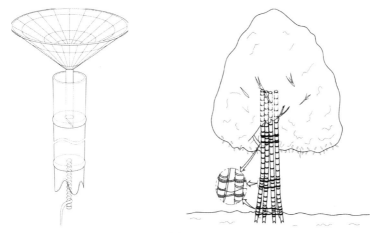

(a) The schematic diagram of the device   (b) Multiple units mounted on a tree to trap rainwater

Figure 10_An eco-friendly method to trap water using bamboo on the hill of a mountain for a specific area behind the perennial snow like the High Atlas Mountain Range in Morocco (Park, 2023)

2.2. Conservation of Groundwater

Like most countries, irrigated agriculture is essential to Morocco's economic and social development. Irrigation accounts for 85% of the total water resources developed to date. Irrigated agriculture is a high priority in Morocco due to its ability to meet the needs of a rapidly growing population and the government's policy to expand exports of produced and processed agricultural products. The expansion of privately developed groundwater-based irrigation has helped minimize the impact of drought and expanded and stabilized farm production. However, in the absence of effective regulatory mechanisms, the rapid increase in private irrigation has resulted in severe aquifer depletion as well as a severe reduction in the flow of several springs and watercourses that support small and medium-scale irrigation peripheries (Doukkali, 2005; Faysse et al. 2012). The decline in groundwater has been accompanied by saltwater intrusion, resulting in salinization of groundwater in some coastal areas. Water resources are also increasingly threatened by pollution. The main sources of pollution are agriculture, industry, and households. Sanitation and wastewater treatment infrastructure has not kept up with the drinking water supply, and urban discharges are now the major source of surface water, groundwater, and coastal pollution (Kadi, 2015). Despite all the efforts and remarkable achievements, Morocco currently faces a growing number of challenges in water management, which, if not managed properly, could hinder the country's economic growth (Kadi & Ziyad, 2018).

Accordingly, more efficient methods of using irrigation water and conserving groundwater should be adopted. First of all, the government must regulate and monitor excessive groundwater exploitation by the private sector. It is necessary to move away from intensive wheat and olive farming using groundwater and adopt new farming methods, such as growing alternative crops that take into account the entire natural ecosystem. In addition, the structure of rivers and streams must be changed, and irrigation systems should be reorganized so that water from the Rif Mountains and Atlas Mountains can flow as slowly as possible. In particular, efficient groundwater conservation methods should be implemented to trap rainwater underground during the rainy season. For example, large water storage tanks installed underground in a river to store water when the river floods or rainwater reservoirs installed underground in parks, parking lots, or rice fields can be alternatives to conserve groundwater. In addition, efforts should be made to prevent groundwater pollution at the source by separating sewers from rivers to block contaminated water from households and industrial facilities by expanding wastewater treatment facilities.

2.3. Securing Absolute Green Space: Restrictions on Cultivation on the Hilly Farmlands and Housing in Mountainous Regions

Centuries of unmanaged forest exploitation have led to the removal of forests, resulting in the loss of biodiversity and land degradation. In particular, forests are often regarded as an ownerless treasure trove of forest products that anyone can freely harvest. Thus, trees are often cut down without considering the long-term effects (Bellefontaine, 2011). Traditional livestock farming is also an important part of the agricultural system. Cattle, sheep, and horses are raised on plains and hillsides where agricultural activities are active, whereas goats are grazed on alpine rangelands. Land clearing reduces the natural vegetation cover of the area and increases the threat of land degradation through soil erosion. The recent changes in agricultural methods have increased these threats. Cultivation and harvesting using traditional methods still dominate. However, mechanization is increasingly introduced where terrain allows agricultural practices, resulting in increased soil loss due to soil compaction and wheeling (Esper et al., 2007).

Thus, it is necessary to restrict any cultivation above 70% of the hilly farmland's height and limit residence in the mountainous regions to ensure absolute green space and protect forests. The biggest challenge, however, is to implement resource utilization and protection policies that reconcile national interests with the interests of local residents. An integrated approach should be implemented that ensures the conservation of the natural environment while providing practicable incentives for local residents and developing re-employment programs for farmers who have lost their jobs. In South Korea, various legislations were enacted to restrict the development of forests and farmland to preserve green space, with successful results.

2.4. Restrictions on the Types of Crops and Tree Species to be Planted

Conservation of biodiversity in the dry lands of Africa is particularly important. Local residents in these regions rely heavily on local biodiversity to meet their daily needs (Davies et al., 2012). However, since the 1990s, tree biodiversity in the Sahel region has been declining at an alarming rate despite reports of increased vegetation cover (Herrmann & Tappan, 2013). Restoring forest landscapes and ecosystems means restoring ecosystem function, which depends on restoring and protecting biodiversity, including the vast numbers of species in the soil, often collectively referred to as "carbon stocks" (Davies, 2017). The United Nations recently released a report on land degradation, analyzing lands around the world that are undergoing restoration from an ecological perspective. The report estimated that nearly half of those lands are planted with fast-growing trees and plants. This type of land restoration means rapid growth of the forest. However, limiting the diversity of plant species also restrains the ecosystem services that naturally restoring forests can provide, such as carbon storage, groundwater recharge, and wildlife habitats (Henderson, 2022).

Similar mistakes can be found in the land restoration project of China. In 1978, recognizing that desertification was associated with the destruction of vegetation and soil erosion rather than the expansion of the Gobi Desert, the Chinese authorities launched a large-scale integrated management project in a vast rectangular area over 4,000 km long and 1,000 km wide. This large-scale project aimed to establish forests in 20% of the total desert area by 2010 (AU-EU, 2009). Although the project received strong political support from the Chinese central government, it encountered many problems at the project site. For example, tree species with little or no adaptation to the local climate and soil were planted, and the diversity of plant species was not taken into consideration, resulting in high mortality rates of planted trees. Scientists emphasize the importance of planting local species (often steppe vegetation) rather than insisting on planting trees with little chance of survival. Therefore, when restoring forests, it is necessary to limit the types of crops and tree species planted to ensure biodiversity. It is recommended to limit fruit trees that are only beneficial to humans, such as olive and orange trees, and to plant species, such as cork trees, which are resistant to dry climate but bears fruit. However, authorities should restrict the removal of the bark from cork trees.

2.5. Democratic Citizenship Education and Environmental Ethics Education for Youth and Citizens

In the top-down decision-making approach, decisions about the location and specifications of a project are made based on the views of policymakers who are not located at the actual site of the project implementation. Thus, the knowledge embedded in the culture and customs of the local community that can assist in the decision-making process is often ignored in the decision-making approach. This can lead to the marginalization of the local residents, which in turn can lead to their apathy towards environmental protection, as they feel that the success of the project is the responsibility of the project initiators rather than their own (Torkar and McGregor, 2012). In the case of the Great Green Wall (GGW) project, this top-down decision-making approach to reforestation efforts ultimately failed (Dok & Berlinger, 2022). The participation of local residents is crucial to achieving the long-term goals of conservation projects or national development. Therefore, a bottom-up decision-making approach should be adopted to encourage voluntary participation from local residents. The foundation lies in civic education and environmental ethics education.

Democratic citizens must fulfill their duties as citizens. They enjoy basic rights and freedoms as individuals but take it for granted that they fulfill the responsibilities and duties of citizenship necessary to maintain the community. The stronger this sense of democratic citizenship is, the stronger a culture of active cooperation with national policies among citizens is formed, enabling long-term sustainable land development. With a heightened sense of social justice, citizens are also more likely to participate in environmental protection activities in various ways. In addition, education on environmental ethics needs to be strengthened so that young people can develop an ethical view of the relationship between the environment and humans. Students should be educated to recognize the environment as a partner that must coexist with humans rather than as an object to be used and exploited for human needs. It is necessary to teach students that caring for and protecting living things is good human behavior.

However, Morocco has not placed citizenship education at the center of public education since independence until now. This opinion is supported by the neglect of social studies education over the past 30 years. As a result, most students do not have a sufficient knowledge foundation to make proper decisions based on public affairs or civic responsibility. In recent years, concerns have been raised in the education fields about the adequacy of the curriculum for democratic citizenship education and the development of necessary human resources. Thus, public education, the cornerstone of democracy and citizenship education, should be central to Morocco's national education program (Ennaji, 2021).

3. Cooperation with International Organizations

National efforts and capacities alone are not enough for sustainable national land development to be successful. It is necessary to utilize international governance to support national land development effectively. A great deal of effort is required to seek cooperation and support from various international organizations. In particular, climate change and environmental issues are of common concern to the world and Africa. The United Nations Development Organization (UNDP) also actively supports sustainable land development internationally. Thus, it is necessary to establish a framework of cooperation with various international organizations, including UNDP, The African-Asian Rural Development Organization (AARDO), The Organisation of African Unity (OAU), and UNESCO. In order to elicit international cooperation and support, it is important to recognize social and environmental justice as the highest priority values to be pursued and to build value-based social and educational systems that can share these values. It will be necessary to strengthen mature citizenship and environmental ethics that can lead to sustainable land development and pursue policies that align with the values of the international community.

4. Bilateral or Multilateral International Cooperation

One of the reasons for Morocco's gradual economic development is its colonial economic exploitation by Western imperialist countries in the past. These imperialist countries prioritized the exploitation of Morocco's resources, and the regional, industrial, and tribal imbalances and divisions that resulted from their domination of Morocco are currently hindering the country's economic development. Thus, the responsibility for causing obstacles to Morocco's development to date also lies with the countries, such as France and Spain, that limited access to education and disproportionately exploited resources during their colonial rule. These countries have a moral responsibility for Morocco's slow economic growth and, thus, have reason and motivation to support

Morocco's economic development more actively. It is necessary to pursue cooperation for sustainable development under the values of democracy and environmental ethics with countries like Spain and France, which are geographically close to Morocco. These countries will likely cooperate with Morocco because Morocco's development will help their economies and environmental challenges.

In particular, it is highly recommended to work with cooperation organizations such as the Korea International Cooperation Agency (KOICA) in South Korea, which not only provides economic support but also shares experiences and know-how on how to overcome the obstacles of colonization and succeed in modernization. It is also necessary to promote cooperation with countries outside of Africa with deserts, such as the United States, China, Mongolia, Uzbekistan, and Kazakhstan. In particular, the United States and China are making great efforts to prevent desertification and efficient land development and have technical experiences that can be shared. Thus, cooperation with these two countries will greatly help promote sustainable development in the future.

V. Conclusion

This study proposes various land development strategies to restore the ecosystems turning into deserts and make efficient use of water resources for sustainable land development in Morocco. As can be seen from many cases of land development in the past, only a harmonious strategy for land redevelopment that considers environmental conservation and economic development together can make Morocco's sustainable land development possible. For a land development strategy to be successful, democratic citizenship education and eco ethics education for citizens that enable citizens to participate in land development voluntarily are just as important as strong leadership of the central government that plans a comprehensive strategy for land development and continuously leads land development.

Sustainable land development is not a short-term project limited to a few regions but a process with long-term goals carried out throughout the country over a long period of time. Thus, it is necessary to establish public enterprises with expertise in land development that will promote national land development consistently and continuously. It is important to note that Korea led land development by establishing public enterprises such as Korea Land Corporation Further efforts should also be made to promote cooperation with international organizations and countries.

Sustainable land development can be achieved through the bottom-up approach that involves local residents of the development sites, not through the top-down decision-making approach of government policies. Democratic citizenship education and eco ethics education build the foundation for a bottom-up approach to national land development. One of the reasons for the failure of environmental restoration projects, including GGW, is the lack of participation from local residents in the projects. Employment support programs should be created for residents who have lost their jobs due to land development, and national education programs to change people's awareness about the environment should be actively implemented. Changing people's awareness about the environment, which can only be built through a long-term educational process, cannot be achieved in a short period of time. Thus, democratic citizenship education and eco ethics education should be central to the national public education curriculum. The proper democratic citizenship education and eco ethics education, especially for youth, will help Morocco become a leader in sustainable development in Africa in the future. In order to create new momentum for change in land development, it would be a good idea to initiate a campaign to reform national social consciousness like the New Community Movement known as "Saemaul Undong," which was implemented during the economic and social modernization of the Republic of Korea. It is widely believed that the main reason countries in the sub-Saharan tropical rainforest region remain in a poor state of affairs is the lack of people's efforts and participation to change to overcome their hardships. Like Morocco, the Republic of Korea has a painful history of colonization by imperialism. However, the nation united to promote the New Community Movement campaign with the mindset of "Let's live well, too," succeeded in modernization, and achieved democratization.

Morocco has high levels of national capacity in many fields and geographical and topographical advantages for land development compared to other African countries. Morocco has sufficient potential to make a successful story in sustainable national development if these conditions are well integrated through effective governance. If Morocco achieves successful land development and shares this experience with neighboring countries, it is expected to have positive synergistic effects on environmental restoration and land development in Africa.

■ References

AU–EU (2009), Etude de préfaisabilité de l'initiative Grande Muraille Verte pour le Sahara et le Sahel + Annexes. African Union-European Union.

Botkin, Daniel B. (1990), *Discordant harmonies: a new ecology for the twenty-first century*, New York: Oxford University Press.

Bell, D. and Carrick, J. (2017), *Procedural environmental justice, The Routledge Handbook of Environmental Justice*, New York: Routledge.

Bellefontaine, R., Bernoux, M., Bonnet, B., Cornet, A., Cudennec, C., D'Aquino, P., & Requier-Desjardins, M. (2023), The African great green wall project: What advice can scientists provide?: A summary of published results. http://www. xn—csfdesertification-nl9j.org/grande%E2%80%90muraille%E2%80%90verte (accessed October 15, 2023).

Berlin, I. (2002), *Two Concepts of Liberty, in I. Berlin, Four Essays on Liberty*, London: Oxford University Press. New ed. in Berlin.

CESE(Conseil Economique, Social et Environnemental) (2014), *La gouvernance par la gestion intégrée des ressources en eau au Maroc:* Levier fondamental de développement durable, Version définitive, Auto-Saisine n 15/2014/.

Davies J, Poulsen L, Schulte-Herbrugen B, Mackinnon K, Crawhall N, Henwood WD, Dudley N, Smith J, Gudka M. (2012), Conserving dryland biodiversity, *International Union for Conservation of Nature,* 08 Sep, 2012.

Davies, J. (2017), *Biodiversity and the Great Green Wall: Managing nature for sustainable development in the Sahel,* IUCN, West and Central Africa Programme (PACO), Ouagadougou, Burkina Faso

Dok, V. G. & Berlinger, P. (2022), The Great Green Wall—Africa's Green World Wonder. *Rural,* 21(2): 26-27.

Doukkali, M. (2005), Water institutional reforms in Morocco. *Water Policy,* 7(1), 71-88.

Ennaji, M. (2021), Multiculturalism, citizenship, and education in Morocco, *Educational Scholarship across the Mediterranean,* 3, 304-325.

Esper, J., Frank, D., Büntgen, U., Verstege, A., Luterbacher, J., & Xoplaki, E. (2007), Long-term drought severity variations in Morocco, *Geophysical research letters,* 34(17),1-5.

Faysse, N., El Amrani, M., El Aydi, S. and Lahlou, A. (2012), 'Formulation and Implementation of Policies to Deal with Groundwater Overuse in Morocco: Which Supporting Coalitions?', *Irrigation and Drainage,* 61(S1), 126-134.

Galtung, J. (1996), *Peace by peaceful means: Peace and conflict, development and civilization,* International Peace Research Institute Oslo; Sage Publications, Inc.

Gellers, Joshua C., and Chris Jeffords (2018), Toward environmental democracy? Procedural environmental rights and environmental justice, *Global Environmental Politics,* 18(1), 99-121.

Goodin, D. K. (2007), Schweitzer reconsidered: The applicability of reverence for life as environmental philosophy, *Environmental Ethics,* 29(4), 403-421.

Habermas, J. (1984), *Vorstudien und Ergänzungen zur Theorie des kommunikativen Handelns*, Frankfurt am Main : Suhrkamp.

Habermas, J. (1962), *The structural transformation of the public sphere: An inquiry into a category of bourgeois society, Thomas Burger, Frederick Lawewnce (trans.).* Cambridge, MA: The MIT Press. ISBN 978-0262581080.

Henderson, B. (2022), The Great Green Wall: Africa's big plan to fight climate change, The Kingfisher. https://www.the-kingfisher.org/sustainable_leaders/africa/african_green_wall.html (accessed October 7, 2023).

Hanich, L., Chehbouni, A., Gascoin, S., Boudhar, A., Jarlan, L., Tramblay, Y.,... & Khabba, S. (2022), Snow hydrology in the Moroccan Atlas Mountains. *Journal of Hydrology: Regional Studies,* 42: 101101.

Herrmann S. M. & Tappan G. G. (2013), Vegetation impoverishment despite greening: a case study from central Senegal, *Journal of Arid Environments,* 90: 55-66.

Kadi, M. A. (2015), ≪The dynamic of water security and sustainable growth≫ opening keynote of the Session on "Economically Water Insecure Countries," VIIth World Water Forum, Gyeongju, South Korea.

Kadi, M. A. & Ziyad, A. (2018), Integrated water resources management in Morocco, *Global Water Security: Lessons Learnt and Long-Term Implications,* 143-163.

Khabba, S., Jarlan, L., Er-Raki, S., Le Page, M., Ezzahar, J., Boulet, G., Simonneaux, V., Kharrou, M.H., Hanich, L., Chehbouni, G. (2013), The SudMed program and the joint international laboratory TREMA: a decade of water transfer study in the soil-plant-atmosphere system over irrigated crops in semi-arid area, *Procedia Environmental Sciences* 19: 524-533. https://doi.org/10.1016/j.proenv.2013.06.059

Hays, Samuel (1959), *Conservations and the Gospel of Efficiency,* Massachusetts: Harvard University Press.

Kandji, S.T.; Verchot, L.; Mackensen, J. (2006), Climate Change and Variability in the Sahel Region: Impacts and Adaptation Strategies in the Agricultural Sector.

Available online: https://www.worldagroforestry.org/publication/climate-change-and-variability-sahel-region-impacts-and-adaptation-strategies (accessed October 10, 2023).

Moçayd, N. E, Suchul Kang, S., and Eltahir, E. (2020), Climate change impacts on the Water Highway project in Morocco, *Hydrology and Earth System Sciences,* 24: 1467-1483.

Molle F. and Tanouti O. (2017), Squaring the circle: Agricultural intensification vs. water conservation in Morocco, *Agricultural Water Management,* 192(C): 170-179.

Notre Dame Global Adaptation Initiative (2023), https://gain.nd.edu/our-work/country-index/ (accessed November 17, 2023).

Park, Gyun Yeol (2023). Water Storage and Supply Control Device Using Bamboo (Utility Model, Korean Intellectual Property Office, Submit No. 20-2023-0002144, 2023.10.20.)

Pinchot, Gifford (1910), *The Fight for Conservation,* New York: Doubleday & Page.

South Korea, 〈Act on Special Measures for Designation and Management of Development Restriction Zones〉

Taylor, P. W. (1986), *Respect for Nature: A Theory of Environmental Ethics,* MA: Princeton University Press.

The Water Diplomat (2022), https://www.waterdiplomat.org/story/2022/03/morocco-water-sector-audit-calls-doubling-efforts (accessed December 7, 2023).

Torkar, G., & McGregor, S. L. T. (2012), Reframing the conception of nature conservation management by transdisciplinary methodology: From stakeholders to stakesharers. *Journal for Nature Conservation* 20(2): 65-71. Doi:10.1016/j.jnc.2011.10.002.

Vizy, E. K. and Cook, K. H. (2012), Mid-Twenty-First-Century Changes in Extreme Events over Northern and Tropical Africa, *Climate,* 25: 5748-5767.

World Bank. 2022, July 20. https://www.worldbank.org/en/news/press-release/2022/07/20/moroccan-economy-slows-in-wake-of-drought-and-commodity-price-rises (accessed December 7, 2023).

Chapter 3

International Cooperation Opportunities in the Moroccan Sahara:
Exploring the Moroccan Autonomy Plan's Potential

Abdellah ACHACH (Researcher in International Law)

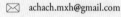 achach.mxh@gmail.com

Dr. Abdellah Achach holds a Ph.D. in International Law from Mohammed V University, Rabat. Prior to his doctoral studies, he earned a Master's degree in international and diplomatic law from the same University and a Bachelor's degree in public law from Moulay Ismail University in Meknes. Dr. Achach also obtained a certificate from the Pakistan Foreign Service Academy *(Islamabad)* following in-depth training on the practice of international relations in addition to a certificate on diplomatic negotiations and Chinese foreign policy, organized in Shanghai by the China-Arab Center for Reform and Development. He also completed a one-year professional training on international relations and diplomacy at the Moroccan Academy of Diplomatic Studies in Rabat. Mr. Achach currently serves as the Economic Counsellor at the Embassy of the Kingdom of Morocco in Seoul. He has previously served as Counsellor in the political section of the Embassy of Morocco in Beijing and Secretary of Foreign Affairs in the Asian Affairs Department at the Moroccan Ministry of Foreign Affairs in Rabat.

I. Introduction

The region that constitutes Morocco has been inhabited since the Paleolithic era, over 300,000 years ago, as evidenced by the discovery of the oldest known Homo sapiens fossils in Morocco in 2017. The first continuous Moroccan state was established by Idris I in 789 (789-978). The country was subsequently ruled by a series of independent dynasties, reaching its zenith as a regional power in the 11th and 12th centuries. These dynasties include the Almoravid Dynasty (1060-1147), the Almohad Dynasty (1145-1248), the Marinid Dynasty (1244-1465), the Saadian Dynasty (1554-1659), and the Alaouite Dynasty, which has ruled the country since 1666 and continues to strengthen the foundations of the modern state. The current King, His Majesty Mohammed VI, is the builder of modern Morocco and the leader of a distinguished approach to the country's development, guided by the same wisdom and patriotic zeal as his esteemed predecessors.

In the 15th and 16th centuries, Morocco faced external threats to its sovereignty but succeeded in being the only North African nation to avoid and resist Ottoman domination (Miller, 2013). Notably, Morocco is one of the few countries in the world to have preserved its independence for over 1,000 years, from the 8th to the 20th century. Additionally, it is one of the first nation-states in the world (IRES, 2019: 42).

- The history of the Kingdom of Morocco is marked by its unique model of colonization and decolonization, distinct from the usual forms experienced by other countries in Africa and around the world.
- 1884: The beginning of Spanish occupation of Morocco's southern cities, starting with the city of Dakhla.
- 1900: The Franco-Spanish Agreement, also known as the Treaty of Paris, which defined the southern and eastern borders of the Rio de Oro.
- 1904: The Convention of Paris, which established the northern border, including the areas of Seguia el-Hamra and Tarfaya, extending to the Wadi Draa.
- In 1912, the Kingdom of Morocco was divided into several zones of occupation: France controlled central Morocco, Spain occupied northern Morocco, as well as the cities of Ceuta and Melilla and the neighboring islands. Spain also controlled southern Morocco (Sakkiat El-Hamra, Oued Eddahab, Tarfaya, and Sidi Ifni), while the international zone of Tangiers was placed under the administration of a council composed of 12 foreign powers. 40 years later, the Kingdom of Morocco began to gradually recover its territorial integrity through negotiated international agreements with the various colonial powers. (Tazi, 2001: 253).
- 1956: Following its independence in 1956, the Kingdom of Morocco

engaged in a series of negotiations with Spain, leading to the gradual recovery of parts of southern Morocco *(IRES, 2023: 14)*.

- Guided by Morocco's doctrine of dialogue and peaceful disputes resolution, agreements were reached for the return of Tarfaya *(1958)* and Sidi Ifni *(1969)* to Morocco, culminating in the Madrid Agreement of 1975. This agreement marked the end of the Spanish presence in the Sahara and was recognized by the United Nations General Assembly in Resolution 3458/B.

- Subsequently, for geopolitical reasons, a neighboring country of Morocco deployed efforts and maneuvers to hinder the full recovery of the Moroccan Sahara, leading to a regional conflict that has persisted for decades.

- Following calls from the UN Security Council to resolve the political deadlock since 2004 *(Amrani, 2021: 13)* Morocco presented the "Moroccan Initiative for Negotiating an Autonomy Status for the Sahara Region" to the UN Secretary-General on April 11, 2007. This initiative guarantees the region's population the right to democratically manage their affairs through legislative, executive, and legal bodies.

In this regard, this paper aims to outline the key features of the Moroccan Autonomy Plan, which has garnered widespread support from the international community, and to highlight the various economic opportunities currently present in the Moroccan Sahara, along with its development aspirations through the aforementioned Autonomy Plan. To this end, the following approach will be adopted:

First, Key Aspects of the Moroccan Autonomy Plan

Second, Current Development Situation in the Moroccan Southern

Provinces

Third, Prospects for International Cooperation in the Moroccan Sahara

II. Key aspects of the Moroccan Autonomy Plan

Following the calls from the UN Security Council for the parties to end the political deadlock that has persisted since 2004, Morocco presented the "Moroccan Initiative for Negotiating an Autonomy Status for the Sahara Region" to the UN Secretary-General on April 11th, 2007. This initiative guarantees to the population of the region the ability to democratically govern their affairs through legislative, executive, and legal bodies.

The Moroccan initiative is significant because it is based on compromise and fully complies with International Law including the UN Charter; the UN Resolutions from both the General Assembly and the Security Council; as well as the right to self-determination.

It is important to note that international law and practice recognize that self-determination can be achieved by acquiring any political status freely agreed upon by the concerned population. Accordingly:

- The "Declaration on Principles of International Law Concerning Friendly Relations and Cooperation Among States in Accordance with the UN Charter" (UNGA Res 2625, 1970) states: "Nothing in the foregoing paragraphs shall be construed as authorizing or encouraging any action which would dismember or impair, totally or in part, the territorial integrity or political unity of sovereign and independent States."

- Resolution 1514 of the UN General Assembly *(1960)* states in its sixth paragraph: "Any attempt aimed at the partial or total disruption of the national unity and the territorial integrity of a country is incompatible with the purposes and principles of the Charter of the United Nations." *(UNGA Res 1514 (XV)*, 1960*)*.

This has been confirmed by many international documents, applications, and analyses. As former UN Secretary-General Boutros Boutros-Ghali emphasized in his "Agenda for Peace"(Boutros-Ghali, 1992: 9) report, "respect for the fundamental sovereignty of the State and its integrity are crucial to any common international progress," warning that "if every ethnic, religious, or linguistic group claimed statehood, there would be no limit to fragmentation, and peace, security, and economic well-being for all would become ever more difficult to achieve."

All of this confirms that the Moroccan Autonomy Plan represents a balanced solution to achieve self-determination without threatening the principle of territorial integrity, consistent with the UN approach that has always prioritized the preservation of state sovereignty and not encouraged fragmentation.

A close reading of the Moroccan Autonomy Plan clearly shows its seriousness, realism, and credibility. The substance of the plan is also distinguished by its coherence with the will of the international community and the applicable international legal and political standards. This initiative allows the principle of self-determination to be realized through a free, democratic, and modern system of self-government. It is in full conformity with international legitimacy, taking into account the applicable global rules and standards regarding self-government, while also ensuring the respect and promotion of human rights as universally recognized and enshrined in the Kingdom's constitution.

In this regard, it is important to note that the High Commission for National Minorities, affiliated with the OSCE (Organization for Security and Cooperation in Europe), created an independent expert group in 1998 to determine the international standards applicable to territorial autonomy.

The expert group held several meetings in Lund (Sweden), resulting in the famous "Lund Recommendations," which provide a guide for the international standards that should be respected when seeking to establish a democratic system of territorial autonomy. The report states that the powers of an autonomous region must include areas such as: education, culture, the use of minority languages, the environment, local and economic development, natural resources, maintaining local order, housing, health, and other social sectors.

As for the Moroccan initiative, the population of the autonomous region exercises its competencies in particular in the following areas:

- Local Administration: Local police and jurisdiction within the region.
- Economy: Economic development, regional planning, encouragement

of investments, trade, industry, tourism, and agriculture.

- Budget and Taxation: The region's budget and taxation.
- Infrastructure: Water management, hydraulic installations, electricity, public construction, and transport.
- Social: Housing, education, health, employment, sport, social security, and protection.
- Culture: Including the promotion of Saharawi cultural heritage.
- Environment: Environmental management.

Therefore, it is clear that the powers granted by the Moroccan Autonomy Plan to the Sahara region are much broader than those recommended by the Lund Report, which excludes regional jurisdiction over areas such as justice, tourism taxation, and transport that must be managed jointly with the central authorities.

III. Current Development Situation in the Moroccan Southern Provinces

Since the recovery of its southern provinces, Morocco has significantly intensified efforts toward the development of these areas, continuing its open development initiatives in the Sahara region.

In this regard, for every dollar of revenue from the region, Morocco invests $7 in the Sahara as part of its policy of solidarity between regions. Regarding Human Development indicators, in 1975, the region was 6% lower than the northern regions of Morocco and 51% lower than the national average in Spain. Today, the indicators in the Sahara region far exceed the averages of other regions in Morocco and neighboring areas.

Currently, the region is known for unprecedented economic and social empowerment. This progress is particularly demonstrated by the launch of the "New Development Plan for the Southern Provinces" by His Majesty King Mohammed VI on November 7, 2015, with a budget of 7.718 billion USD (Vedie, 2023: 1), which has allowed for the creation of 120,000 new job opportunities.

It is also worth noting that the Moroccan government has been strengthening infrastructure in the southern cities, carrying out a series of large-scale projects in recent years to position the region as a key investment destination. These initiatives have included industrial parks, free zones, and transport networks, all aimed at further developing the local economy and creating a favorable environment for private investment beyond the region.

The stability of Morocco and the investment opportunities provided by the southern regions of the Kingdom explain the increasing number of countries that have opened consular representations in the region, with more than 30 consulates in Laayoune and Dakhla, established by countries from all over the world.

For example, Dakhla-Oued Eddahab, one of the southern provinces of Morocco, covers 18.4% of the Kingdom's area and occupies a strategic location in the south, acting as a bridge between Morocco and Europe via the Atlantic Ocean, as well as between Morocco and sub-Saharan

Africa through Mauritania.

Regarding GDP per capita, the Sahara region's is 1.6 times higher than the national average. In particular, the GDP per capita of the Dakhla region is more than double the national average, with the region's gross income per capita growing at one of the highest rates in the country, at 5.8% per year.

Dakhla is one of the most promising economic hotspots in Africa for businesses seeking to strengthen commercial ties between Europe and West Africa. This role will be further enhanced by the flagship Dakhla Atlantic Port mega-project, which is slated to be completed by 2028. The port will feature a deep commercial port, a coastal and deep-sea fishing port, shipbuilding facilities, and industrial and logistics zones.

In addition to Dakhla Atlantic Port, the Moroccan government is developing two 30-hectare logistics platforms at the border posts of El Guerguerat and Bir Guendouz to support the region's efforts to position itself as a key access point for Africa and an important trade center.

Politically, it is worth noting that legislative, regional, and municipal elections are consistently held in a calm and orderly manner, with massive participation from the two regions of the Moroccan Sahara. In the most recent elections, the turnout rate exceeded 66%, demonstrating the region's commitment to its Moroccan identity and to the democratic process.

In this regard, two Saharawi citizens were elected as Presidents of the two Sahara regions, alongside the presidents and members of the regional and municipal councils, all of whom are from the region. These elections enable the region to renew its political elites, who will continue managing and planning the development efforts within the framework of the New Development Model for the Southern Provinces.

IV. Prospects for International Cooperation in the Moroccan Sahara

It is worth noting that the Moroccan government has been the largest investor and employer in the Southern Provinces since the region's recovery in 1975. Investment primarily focuses on high-priority social sectors and far exceeds the provinces' revenues from mining and fishery resources.

- From 1975 to 2013, Morocco invested approximately 120 billion MAD (12 billion USD) in infrastructure, including administration, communications and telecommunications, electricity and water, education, housing, and health.
- 2013 marked a turning point when His Majesty King Mohammed VI launched the New Development Model for the Southern Provinces, with a budget of 77 billion MAD (7 billion USD) dedicated to key infrastructure projects.
- The Southern Provinces are transitioning from a resource-based economy to a competitive economy under the New Development Model, creating an environment conducive to private investment, which is expected to become the main driver of wealth and employment.

- Since the launch of the 2016-2025 program, several major private players have committed to investing a total of MAD 6 billion (600 million USD) in approximately 60 projects.
- In terms of foreign investment, operators from about thirty countries are present in the Southern Provinces, including international banks.

Seven years later, significant achievements have been made, including the completion of the Tiznit-Dakhla expressway (Sissao, 2021: 58) -which is 1.55 Kilometers long and considerably reducing the duration and cost of transport- the connection of the southern regions to the national electricity grid, the enhancement of communication networks, and the establishment of solar and wind power stations. The Dakhla Atlantic Port construction project, with a completion rate of 27% by November 2024 (Northafricapost, 2024), is progressing rapidly. Full completion is expected in 2028, with terminal operations set to begin in 2029.

In addition to the Autonomy Plan, which aims to consolidate the aforementioned progress while providing the necessary financial resources for the region's development, another Royal initiative was launched on November 6th, 2023, during the 48th anniversary of the Green March. His Majesty the King announced the "Royal Initiative for the Atlantic," through which Morocco proposes to open its maritime access via the port of Dakhla to landlocked Sahelian countries such as Mali, Niger, Burkina Faso, and Chad.

In His speech on this occasion, His Majesty the King emphasized the importance of:

- Morocco's ongoing pursuit of development and modernization policies, including in the Moroccan Sahara, where the recovery of the southern provinces has enhanced the country's Atlantic dimension and strengthened its international standing.
- Rehabilitating Morocco's national coastline, especially the section of the Moroccan Sahara bordering the Atlantic Ocean.
- Transforming the region into a vibrant hub for human interaction and economic integration, playing a pivotal role at both the continental and international levels.
- Improving transportation, logistics platforms, and the development of a competitive national commercial marine fleet to foster connectivity between countries bordering the Atlantic.

In line with His Majesty the King's vision, the Southern Provinces of Morocco will act as a bridge between Morocco and Europe via the Atlantic Ocean, and between Morocco and sub-Saharan Africa through Mauritania. The development of infrastructure and connectivity to existing transport and communication networks is expected to catalyze fundamental economic transformations in the Sahel countries and the region as a whole, as demonstrated by projects like the Morocco-Nigeria gas pipeline, which aims to promote regional integration and stimulate joint economic growth.

All of this leads us to the central question of this paper: What are the opportunities for international cooperation offered by the Moroccan Sahara in light of the Moroccan Autonomy Plan?

In light of the above-mentioned elements, it is important to note that Morocco's southern Saharan provinces are becoming increasingly attractive to numerous international investors seeking to capitalize on the opportunities these regions offer. Morocco continues to make substantial investments in infrastructure, including the Dakhla Atlantic Port, which aims to be the "Tangier Med" for the southern region, fostering stronger trade ties with Africa and the world.

Other projects in the region include the completion of a nearly 1,000 km-long multi-lane highway connecting Agadir city to Dakhla in the South. Additionally, the borders with Mauritania have been expanded to facilitate the transportation of goods to neighboring southern countries. The Dakhla region, located on the Atlantic coast, holds immense potential in the fishing industry, tourism, renewable energy production, and as a transshipment point for trade to Africa. In this context, different countries, including the Republic of Korea, stand to benefit from the economic opportunities presented by the development initiatives in this region.

This new vision shifts the Moroccan Sahara from a local economic dimension based on interconnectedness to a new dimension in which the Sahara region will transform into an engine that drives the economies of the Sahel countries, opening them up to the Atlantic.

Boosting infrastructure across the Atlantic coastline would create an integrated economy based on offshore natural resource exploration, marine fishing investment, and seawater desalination, which would invigorate agricultural activities and support renewable energy as key aspects of the region's development.

The rapid transformations the world is experiencing, especially the strategic challenges facing the Afro-Atlantic space, prompted Morocco to choose the Atlantic coast as a launchpad for joint cooperation with the Americas. This strategy is aimed at strengthening Africa's Atlantic coast, opening its gates, and preparing it to play a more advanced and decisive role in defending recent gains.

The Moroccan Sahara offers, today, various opportunities for international cooperation across a range of fields. These opportunities are shaped by the region's economic potential and its strategic position. Here are some key areas of international cooperation in the region:

- Renewable Energy: The Moroccan Sahara has vast potential for renewable energies, particularly solar and wind power, thanks to its expansive sunny landscapes, making it an attractive location for international partners in large-scale energy projects. Among the biggest projects are the Noor solar power plant, located near the town of Ouarzazate on the edge of the Sahara, and the Tarfaya wind farm -the largest in Africa- located on the Atlantic coast, with more than 130 wind turbines and a total capacity of 301 MW (MRS). Morocco is also one of the most promising locations for offshore wind energy in Africa, with the potential to generate up to 200 GW.
- Infrastructure Development: The region has significant potential for international partnerships in infrastructure development, such as roads, ports, and airports. The region's strategic location near the Atlantic Ocean and its proximity to Europe make it a key hub for trade and

transportation. Notable projects include the New Dakhla Atlantic Port, the West Africa industrial and logistics zone, the Dakhla-Tiznit expressway, and desalination stations.

- Blue Economy: The blue economy holds substantial potential to create jobs (currently generating nearly 50 million jobs across Africa), in addition to employment in sectors like fisheries, maritime shipping, and coastal tourism. The Moroccan Sahara's potential in fisheries and maritime shipping is significant, benefiting from active investments as part of the government's program focusing on economic development, jobs, food security, and natural resource management, supported by the World Bank's Blue Economy Program for Results (PforR).

- Desertification and Land Management: Morocco is actively engaged in international climate initiatives. The Sahara region offers opportunities for joint efforts in combating desertification, managing arid landscapes, and preserving biodiversity. International agencies and NGOs could collaborate on sustainable land management, afforestation, and water conservation projects.

- Biodiversity Conservation: The Moroccan Sahara is home to unique species and ecosystems. International cooperation on wildlife preservation, biodiversity conservation, and ecotourism is an area of growing interest.

- Tourism Development: Given the Sahara's mystique and natural beauty, there is significant potential for international partnerships in tourism development, ranging from eco-tourism to adventure tourism. Such projects could also emphasize sustainable tourism practices, ensuring the region's preservation for future generations.

- Border Security and Migration: Cooperation on managing migration routes through the Sahara and addressing border security is another area where Morocco can collaborate with international bodies, including the European Union, the United Nations, and neighboring African nations.

- Research Collaboration: The Moroccan Sahara offers unique opportunities for scientific research, particularly in fields like geology, climate science, and desert ecosystems. International universities and research institutions can collaborate on projects studying desert environments, the effects of climate change, and sustainable living in arid regions.

- Educational Exchange: Collaboration in education, particularly in environmental science, engineering, and international relations, can also be encouraged. Morocco's universities can partner with international institutions to create exchange programs and joint research initiatives.

- Agricultural Innovation: The harsh climate conditions of the Sahara require innovative agricultural techniques, such as hydroponics or drought-resistant crops. Partnerships with international experts and organizations could lead to the development of new methods that benefit the region and provide solutions for other desert areas globally.

V. Conclusion

The Moroccan Autonomy Plan evidently encompasses all the essential elements of seriousness, credibility, and realism, principles consistently underscored by UN Security Council resolutions, which have played a pivotal role in fostering its growing international support.

Indeed, for decades, Morocco has been actively fostering development and progress in its southern regions, which now serve as an essential foundation for the Autonomy Plan. This initiative promises to further accelerate the development of the Moroccan Sahara, while simultaneously promoting stability and integration across the region.

In conclusion, international cooperation in the Moroccan Sahara offers tremendous opportunities for economic growth, environmental sustainability, and cultural exchange. By capitalizing on the region's unique potential, Morocco is clearly able to drive mutual progress and stability, benefiting the entire region.

■ References

Amrani, Y. (2021) Moroccan Sahara: Understand the roots and dynamics of the regional dispute, Embassy the Kingdom of Morocco in South Africa.

Besnard, J. (2013) Rethinking the Sahara dispute, history and contemporary perspectives, AUSACO, 2021.

Boutros B.G. (1992) *An Agenda for Peace, preventive diplomacy, peacemaking and peacekeeping*, Report of the Secretary-General pursuant to the statement adopted by the Summit Meeting of the UN Security Council on 31 January 1992.

Susan Gilson Miller, A History of Modern Morocco, Cambridge: Cambridge University Press.

Tazi, A. (2001), *the mediator in Morocco's international history*, volume III,

The Royal Institute for Strategic Studies (December 2019) panorama of Morocco in the world, the Kingdom's International Relations, IRES.

The Royal Institute for Strategic Studies, (June 2023), The White Book on Moroccan Sahara, IRES.

UNGA, (1960) Resolution 1514 (XV), United Nations General Assembly, 14 December 1960

UNGA, (1970) Resolution 2625 of the United Nations General Assembly, 24 October 1970

Vedie, H.L (2023), The New Development Model of the Southern Provinces: Achievements at a sustained pace reaching the set objectives, https://www. policycenter.ma.

Chapter 4

Moroccan Geographical Characteristics and Natural Disasters

Jongnam Choi (Western Illinois University)

✉ choijnam@hotmail.com

Dr. Jongnam Choi is a Professor in the Department of Earth, Atmospheric, and Geographic Information Sciences at Western Illinois University. He teaches meteorology, climate change, and quantitative geography. His research interests emerge at the intersection of climate, weather, and human well-being. His recent research project includes climate changes in Northeast Asia and the impact of rainfall in subtropical forests using remotely sensed data and CO_2 emission. He is an author/editor of atlases, books, and book chapters such as The Handy Weather Answer Book, The National Atlas of Korea, The Geography of Korea, and The Geography of Dokdo. He also contributes to many journals and encyclopedias.

I. Introduction

Morocco, known for its striking landscapes and diverse climate zones, has faced significant natural disaster challenges in recent years. The country's unique geography, straddling the Atlantic Ocean, the Mediterranean Sea, and the Sahara Desert, makes it vulnerable to a variety of natural hazards. Over the years, Morocco has endured a range of catastrophic events, from earthquakes and floods to prolonged droughts. These disasters not only threaten the lives and livelihoods of its citizens but also exert substantial pressure on its economy, which relies heavily on agriculture, tourism, and natural resources.

The recent 6.8 magnitude earthquake in September 2023 caused widespread destruction, particularly in rural areas where infrastructure is fragile, revealing gaps in preparedness and resilience. In addition to seismic activity, the country grapples with unpredictable weather patterns driven by climate change. Flash floods, such as those that devastated parts of Marrakech and surrounding regions in recent years, are becoming increasingly frequent, washing away homes, roads, and crops. Droughts are also taking a toll, leading to water shortages and threatening agricultural productivity, which is the backbone of Morocco's rural economy.

As the Moroccan economy continues to grow, it faces the urgent challenge of balancing economic growth with the need for sustainable disaster management and climate adaptation strategies. Understanding the interplay between these natural hazards and human activities is crucial for designing effective policies to mitigate their impact. This study aims to briefly describe Morocco's geographical environment and how this environment influences its climatic conditions, explore the causes of natural disasters and their impact geographically, assess current response frameworks, and propose solutions to enhance the nation's socioeconomic resilience and environmental sustainability in the face of an increasingly unpredictable future environment.

II. Morocco's Geography and Climate

Morocco, located in the northwestern corner of Africa, is a land of diverse landforms and contrasting climates. Bordered by the Atlantic Ocean to the west and the Mediterranean Sea to the north, Morocco encompasses coastal plains, towering mountain ranges, expansive deserts, and lush river valleys, each contributing to its unique climatic conditions and ecological richness (Figure 1).

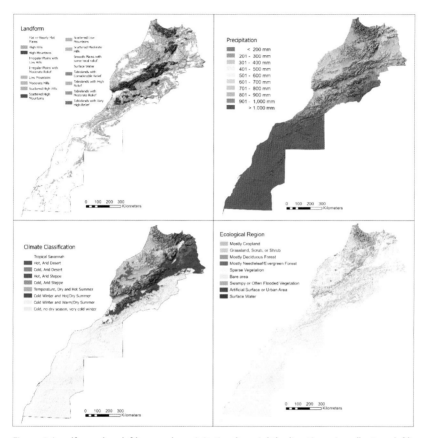

Figure 1. Landforms (top left), annual precipitation (top right), climatic regions (bottom left), and ecological regions (bottom right) in Morocco. **Source:** World Ecological Facets Landform Classes, WorldClim Global Mean Precipitation, Koppen-Geiger Climate Classification, and European Space Agency Climate Change Initiative-Land Cover 2018, respectively.

The Atlas Mountains, the Middle Atlas, the High Atlas, and the Anti-Atlas, run diagonally through the country and form a natural barrier dividing Morocco into distinct climatic zones. These mountains not only shape Morocco's weather patterns but also influence its hydrology, as they capture moisture from the Atlantic, feeding rivers and groundwater resources essential for agriculture and human consumption. Snow-capped summits in the High Atlas range provide a source of meltwater critical during the dry summer months (Figure 1).

The Sahara Desert lies to the southeast of the Atlas Mountains. This markedly arid region experiences extreme temperatures, with scorching summers and cold, windy winters. In stark contrast, Morocco's coastal areas enjoy a Mediterranean climate characterized by mild, wet winters and hot, dry summers. The coastal plains are some of the most productive agricultural zones in the country, benefiting from moderate temperatures and reliable rainfall (Figure 1).

However, Morocco's diverse geography also brings a range of climatic challenges. The interior regions, particularly the semi-arid plateaus and the pre-Saharan zones, often suffer from prolonged droughts, while the mountainous areas are prone to flash floods during the rainy season. These extreme weather events are becoming more frequent and severe due to the impacts of climate change, which poses a significant threat to Morocco's natural resources, agricultural productivity, and rural livelihoods. The country's water resources, largely dependent on seasonal rains and snowmelt, are increasingly strained as rainfall patterns become more erratic. The interaction between Morocco's geography and its climate has shaped not only its ecosystems but also its historical development, influencing patterns of settlement, agriculture, and trade.

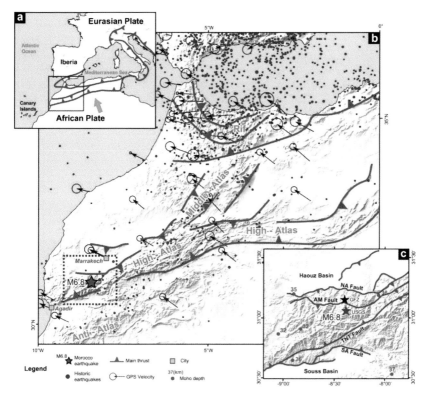

Figure 2. Seismotectonic background of the M_w 6.8 earthquake in Morocco on 8 September 2023. (From: Huang, K., et.al, (2024). https://doi.org/10.1029/2024GL109052)

III. Earthquakes

Morocco is located in a seismically active region. Morocco's seismic activity is primarily driven by its location near the convergent boundary between the African and Eurasian plates (Figure 2). Its proximity to the complex tectonic boundary between these two plates results in periodic earthquakes. This zone stretches across the Mediterranean region, including North Africa and southern Europe. The African plate is moving northward towards the Eurasian plate at a rate of about 4-6 mm per year. This slow but steady movement, as a consequence of subduction-related processes (Gutscher et al., 2012; Platt et al., 2013), produces compressional forces along faults in the region, which lead to interpolated earthquakes along the boundaries of tectonic plates. Several major faults crisscross in Morocco particularly in the Rif and Atlas Mountains, a zone of active crustal deformation, resulting from the tectonic compression, where stress from the converging plates is released along ancient faults. Figure 2 shows major faults in Morocco, including the Tizi N'Test (TNT) Fault through the High Atlas region, the South Atlas Fault at the southern edge of the Atlas range,

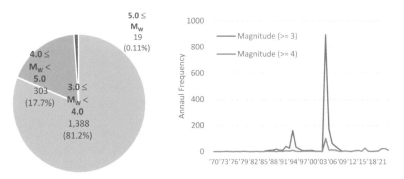

Figure 3. (Left) Percentage of earthquakes by magnitude and (right) annual frequency of Earthquakes year by magnitude (1970-2023). **Source:** USGS.gov.

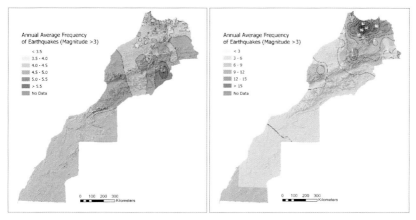

Figure 4. Annual average frequency of Earthquakes in Morocco at magnitudes of 3.0 or higher and 4.0 or higher. **Source:** USGS.gov

and the Middle Atlas Fault System and the Rif Mountains. In addition, the varied geological structure, including mountainous terrain and sedimentary basins, often amplifies seismic impacts in certain areas, leading to more intense damage.

Morocco experiences mostly moderate earthquakes, ranging from magnitude 3.0 to 5.0 (Figure 3). These earthquakes are mostly non-destructive. Earthquakes with a magnitude of 5.5 or higher are less common but occur occasionally. Morocco does not face earthquakes as frequently as other regions in the Mediterranean countries.

Figure 4 shows the geographic distribution of the annual average frequencies of earthquakes at magnitudes greater than 3.0 and 4.0 for the period of 1970 and 2023 in Morocco. The high number of earthquake outbreaks in particular years, such as 1994, 2004, and 2005, may distort the earthquake frequency map. Given that, the most seismically active area in Morocco is the north region, particularly along the Rif Mountains and coastal areas around Al Hoceima and Nador. This area lies close to the tectonic boundary where the African Plate converges with the

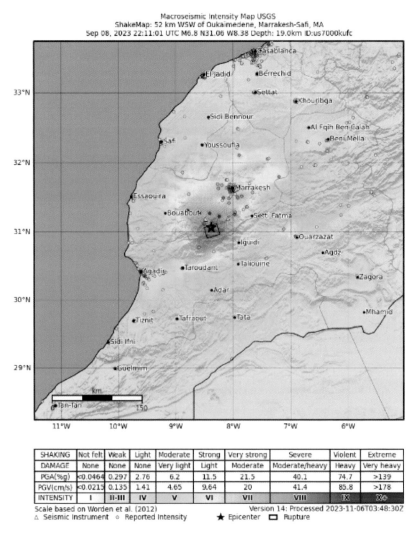

Figure 5. Macroseismic Intensity Map (right) of the 6.8 magnitude earthquake on September 8, 2023. From: USGS.gov

Eurasian Plate, making it highly susceptible to earthquakes. The High Atlas and Middle Atlas Mountain ranges in central Morocco are also prone to earthquakes, though less frequently than the northern regions. The most recent damaging earthquake, the Al Haouz Earthquake, occurred in Al Haouz province near Marrakech on September 8, 2023. This powerful 6.8 magnitude earthquake resulted in over 2,900 deaths, thousands of injuries, and billions of dollars in damages. It also damaged numerous historical sites in the old city including a UNESCO World Heritage site and destroyed thousands of homes in the surrounding rural areas (Figure 5). This earthquake highlighted the vulnerability of this area, especially remote and mountainous communities with poorly constructed buildings (Caputo and Vicari, 2024). Western Coastal Regions like Agadir are also at risk. While earthquakes are less frequent here compared to the north, they can be particularly destructive due to the higher population density and infrastructure, as demonstrated by the catastrophic 1960 earthquake with a magnitude of 5.8 that occurred in Agadir, a city located on Morocco's Atlantic coast. This earthquake resulted in around 12,000 deaths, many more injuries, and over 35,000 homeless. On the other hand, earthquakes are less frequent in the interior regions.

Considering the combination of tectonic activity, vulnerable infrastructure, and densely populated regions, future major earthquakes will pose a substantial threat to the country's social and economic stability. The Moroccan government has improved its network of seismic monitoring stations managed by the National Center for Scientific and Technical Research (CNRST). To minimize damage from future earthquakes, it is necessary for the Moroccan government to improve its disaster response capabilities, focusing on early warning systems, emergency response training, and public awareness campaigns. Most importantly, it is necessary to strictly enforce existing building codes and implement new urban planning to reduce risks from earthquakes and to improve earthquake resilience in more vulnerable regions, especially in rural areas where many homes are still built using traditional materials.

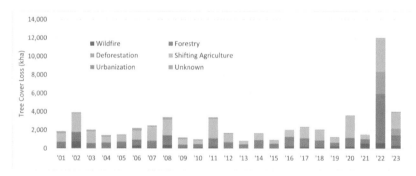

Figure 6. Tree cover loss (kha) from 2001 to 2023. **Source:** Global Forest Watch

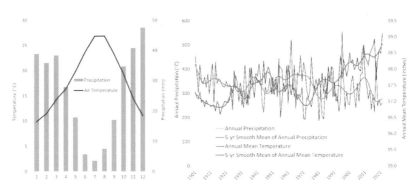

Figure 7. (Left) Monthly mean air temperature and mean precipitation (1991-2020) (left) **Source:** Climate Change Knowledge Portal and (Right) Changes in annual mean temperature and annual precipitation in Morocco (1901-2022). **Source:** Climate Change Knowledge Portal

IV. Floods

Floods are the recurring natural disasters in Morocco. This topography greatly contributes to floods. The Atlas Mountains run through the center of Morocco, forming a natural divide between the Mediterranean northern coastal zone and the southern interior regions, which lie on the edge of the Sahara Desert. Rainwater on the windward side and sudden snowmelt on the northern slope of the mountain ranges contribute to flooding. Deforestation and land degradation reduce the land's natural ability to absorb water and increase runoff and soil erosion (Figure 6).

There has been an increase in both the frequency and intensity of flood events due to more extreme and unpredictable weather patterns driven by climate change. Rising temperatures due to recent global warming have intensified the hydrological cycle, leading to more intense and irregular rainfall events and increasing the risk of flash floods

(Figure 7 Right; Chaqdid et.al., 2023). Floods are most common during the rainy season, which typically runs from November to March (Figure 7 Left). Intense flash floods frequently occur in the Atlas Mountains and the surrounding valleys. These floods are often caused by heavy rains that quickly overwhelm riverbeds and seasonal riverbeds (dry wadis), leading to rapid and destructive flows. The flood of southern Morocco in November 2014, centered in the Anti-Atlas region of Guelmin, was triggered by intense rainfall. Urban floods often occur every 2 to 3 years and cause significant damage, particularly in urban areas (Départment du Developpement Durable, Morocco, 2021).

On September 7 and 8, 2024, an extratropical cyclone brought heavy rainfall to the Moroccan Sahara (Rieder *et al.*, 2024). The resulting runoff created flash floods, overflowing river banks and inundating surrounding areas. This study monitors the flood using the Normalized Difference Water Index (NDWI), which is widely used in remote sensing to monitor and measure the amount of moisture in vegetation and surface water bodies. This index can quantify the presence and concentration of water in liquid and vapor forms within plants as well as water on the surface of the Earth (Gao, 1996). When visualized, NDWI values can map the changes in surface water and the extent of flooding (McFeeters, 1996). When interpreting NDWI values, higher values indicate a greater presence of water, with a scale generally ranging from -1 to +1, where positive values represent water bodies and vegetation with high moisture content, while negative values indicate dry areas like bare soil or built-up surfaces.

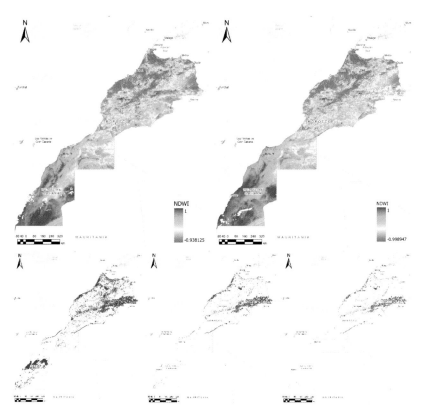

Figure 8. The NDWI values across Morocco (Top Left) before (August 14, 2024) and (Top Right) after (September 10, 2024) the heavy rainfall event on September 7-8, 2024. The regions showing a positive difference in NDWI values before and after the rainfall event at the ranges of 0.05-1.00 (Bottom Left), 0.10-1.00 (Bottom Center), and 0.15-1.00 (Bottom Right)

This study used Band 4 (Green; 0.545-0.565 mm) and Band 5 (NIR; 1.230-1.250 mm) of the MODIS (Moderate Resolution Imaging Spectroradiometer) on NASA's Terra satellite to calculate the NDWI values. These MODIS band datasets provide surface reflectance at a 500-meter spatial resolution. This study compares the NDWI values after (September 10, 2024) and before (August 14, 2024) the heavy rainfall event to delineate the extent of the flooded areas and the intensity of floods (Figure 8). Areas with positive values are those where surface water has increased through heavy rainfall events. This study assumes that areas, where NDWI values increase above a certain value, are either flooded or partially flooded due to this rainfall event. The Daar River and its flood plains, which were flooded by this heavy rainfall event, show distinctly positive values. Figure 8 shows the areas with positive differences in NDWI values at three different ranges of 0.05-1.00, 0.10-1.00, and 0.15-1.00. The areas that showed positive values at those ranges are 20,274 km^2, 3,957 km^2, and 2,065 km^2, respectively. However, these values are estimated area using satellite images. A process of comparing the values in the satellite images with actual surface observations is necessary to verify the accuracy of satellite imagery interpretation and to ensure that the data interpreted from the images accurately reflects the flooded conditions. Once this ground truthing is achieved, it would be possible to model the potential flood area when assuming that twice or three times the amount of rain precipitates in the same area.

Floods lead to extensive economic losses and environmental damage, affecting industries and businesses in urban areas and crop damage and soil erosion in agricultural regions. The Moroccan government has invested in modernizing flood mitigation infrastructure, such as the construction of dams and reservoirs to control water flow, enhancement of early warning systems for flash floods, and improvement of urban drainage systems. Further efforts should be made to implement urban planning to reduce flood risks in urban regions and reforestation with sustainable agricultural practices to reduce runoff and land degradation in rural regions.

V. Droughts

Droughts in Morocco are a persistent and intensifying challenge over the past several decades. Vizy and Cook (2012) predicted that the northern part of Africa is more likely to suffer from an increase in temperature and a decrease in the amount and frequency of precipitation due to the recent climate change. According to the global-scale drought risk assessment for agricultural systems (Meza et.al., 2020), Morocco ranked the fourth highest in the world. Morocco is also recognized as vulnerable to climate change impacts due to its combination of geographic and social factors (Notre Dame Global Adaptation Initiative, 2023). Morocco is among the world's most water-stressed countries (World Bank, 2022).

Droughts in Morocco are closely tied to the variability of its Mediterranean climate, characterized by hot, dry summers (Figures 1 and 7). Historically, Morocco experiences a significant drought every 3 to 5 years. Since the 1980s, there has been a noticeable increase in the frequency, with droughts now occurring almost every 2 to 3 years.

Droughts are now occurring almost twice as often as they did in the early 20th century. Many of these droughts last multiple years.

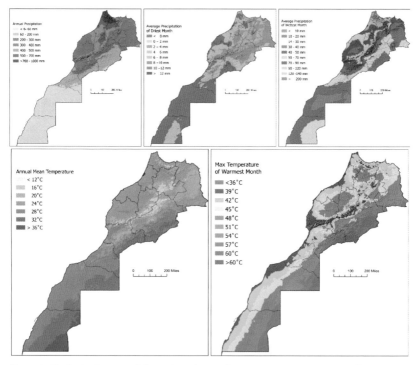

Figure 9. Clockwise from top-left: projected annual precipitation, precipitation of wettest month (December), precipitation of driest month (July), max temperature of warmest month (July), and annual mean temperature in 2050. These maps are based on the IPCC climate scenario (SSP3-8.5 scenario) and its indicators. SSP = Shared Socioeconomic Pathway.
Source: WorldClime CMIP6 Bioclimate

Over the period between 1961 and 2017, cumulative rainfall decreased by 16%, most notably in spring (down 43%) and winter (down 26%) (Départment du Developpement Durable, Morocco, 2021; The World Bank Group, 2021). However, the geographical location and season greatly determine the change in precipitation at the regional level. Decreasing precipitation is particularly pronounced in the southern part of Morocco. Climate models show that this trend continues under all greenhouse gas emission pathways (Figure 9). The decrease in mean annual precipitation is projected to continue in Morocco. The decline ranges from 10% to 20% over the period 2036-2065 compared with 1981-2018, although there will be regional variability (Départment du Developpement Durable, Morocco, 2021). Over the long term, projections show 30% less precipitation in the central part of the country. Decreasing precipitation is raising concerns about droughts, which have increased in frequency, intensity, and duration. Climate projections show more frequent and severe droughts, especially in the central and southern regions (Figure 9).

The average temperature across Morocco has seen an increase of 0.2°C per decade. It rose by 1.7° C between 1971 and 2017 (Départment du Developpement Durable, Morocco, 2021; The World Bank Group, 2021). Climate models show that this trend continues under all greenhouse gas emission pathways. Based on the Shared Socioeconomic Pathway SSP 4.5 scenario, a medium level of greenhouse gas concentration, an additional 1.5°C to 1.8°C increase in the average annual temperature is projected by 2050, compared with the reference period of 1981-2018. Under a high-emissions scenario (SSP 8.5), the average annual temperature will rise between 2°C to 3°C (Figure 9).

Although droughts affect the entire country, their impact varies by region. Central and Southern Morocco are characterized by limited rainfall due to their arid climates (Figures 1 and 9). These regions are among the most severely affected by droughts because of substantial reductions in water availability due to further declining rainfall in recent years. Thus, drought is a chronic issue in these regions. Droughts also occur in the northern coastal region during prolonged dry spells.

Morocco has been hit by major droughts in the early 1980s, mid-1990s, 2000s, and several times over the last decade. Climate change, unsustainable water management practices, and increased water demand have contributed to the frequency, intensity, and spatial extent of droughts in recent years. Rising temperatures and reduced rainfall due to climate change led to longer and more intense droughts. Intensive agriculture has led to significant declines in water tables, resulting in drought, especially in regions where groundwater is heavily used for irrigation (Molle and Tanouti, 2017). Land degradation, driven by deforestation, overgrazing, and unsustainable farming practices, reduces the soil's ability to retain moisture, exacerbating the impact of droughts (Figure 6). In addition, increasing water demand for domestic and industrial use due to population growth and urbanization has strained the limited water resources, particularly in urban areas.

The National Water Plan will greatly improve its water resource management and ensure the nation's long-term water sustainability by expanding of water infrastructure and promoting efficient irrigation techniques. The Green Morocco Plan will further reduce the vulnerability to droughts by encouraging farmers to adopt drought-resistant crops and implement climate-resilient farming practices and sustainable water-saving techniques. However, further efforts should be made to restore degraded land, increase forest cover, and harvest rainwater.

VI.Conclusion

Morocco is increasingly vulnerable to the impacts of climate change, which is expected to exacerbate floods and droughts. This study has examined the multifaceted impacts of natural disasters in Morocco, emphasizing the critical role of its diverse geography and climate in shaping the nation's vulnerability to earthquakes, floods, and droughts. Morocco's susceptibility to earthquakes is largely tied to its tectonic setting, with significant risks in densely populated northern regions. Floods have been exacerbated by climate change and human activity, such as deforestation, urbanization, and more importantly erratic rainfall due to climate change. Droughts have been increasing in frequency. The growing threat of droughts is driven by the reduction in precipitation due to climate change and the increase in water consumption.

The increasing frequency and intensity of these events underscore the urgency of implementing comprehensive mitigation strategies to enhance resilience and sustainability. Disaster management frameworks must address the scale and complexity of these natural disasters. Morocco can reduce vulnerability to natural disasters by adopting a holistic approach that balances immediate disaster preparedness with long-term climate adaptation and the bottom-up, community-based approach that involves residents of areas with frequent natural disasters. Morocco's success in facing the nation's imminent natural disasters can be a global dialogue on addressing natural disasters in the context of climate change and environmental sustainability.

■ References

Caputo, R. and Vicari, A., The 8 September 2023, MW 6.8, Morocco earthquake: A deep transpressive faulting along the active high Atlas mountain belt. Geophysical Research Letters, 51(2), (2024). https://doi.org/10.1029/2023GL106992

Chaqdid A., Alexandre Tuel A., Fatimy A., and Moçayd N., Extreme rainfall events in Morocco: Spatial dependence and climate drivers, Weather and Climate Extremes, 40 (2023) https://doi.org/10.1016/j.wace.2023.100556

Départment du Developpement Durable, Morocco, *4éme Quartriéme Communication Nationale du Maroc: à la Convention Cadre des Nations Unies sur les Changements Climatiques*, (2021) https://unfccc.int/sites/default/files/resource/Quatri%C3%A8me%20Communication%20Nationale_MOR.pdf

Elkharrim, M., L. and Bahi. 2014. Using Statistical Downscaling of GCM Simulations to Assess Climate Change Impacts on Drought Conditions in the Northwest of Morocco, *Modern Applied Science*, 9(2), 1-11 (2014)

Ellero, A., Malusà, M., Ottria, G., Ouanaimi, H., & Froitzheim, N., Transpressional structuring of the high Atlas belt, Morocco, *Journal of Structural Geology*, 135,

104021 (2020) https://doi.org/10.1016/j.jsg.2020.104021

Gao, B. C. (1996). NDWI—A normalized difference water index for remote sensing of vegetation liquid water from space. *Remote sensing of environment, 58*(3), 257-266 (1996). https://doi.org/10.1016/S0034-4257(96)00067-3

Global Forest Watch, https://www.globalforestwatch.org/dashboards/country/MAR/?category=fires

McFeeters, S. K. (1996). The use of the Normalized Difference Water Index (NDWI) in the delineation of open water features. *International journal of remote sensing, 17*(7), 1425-1432 (1996). https://doi.org/10.1080/01431169608948714

Meza, I., Siebert, S., Döll, P., Kusche, J., Herbert, C., Eyshi Rezaei, E., Nouri, H., Gerdener, H., Popat, E., Frischen, J., Naumann, G., Vogt, J. V., Walz, Y., Sebesvari, Z., and Hagenlocher, M., Global-scale drought risk assessment for agricultural systems, Nat. Hazards Earth Syst. Sci., 20, 695-712, https://doi.org/10.5194/nhess-20-695-2020, 2020.

Notre Dame Global Adaptation Initiative, (2023, November 12), https://gain.nd.edu/our-work/country-index/

Rieder, J., Aemisegger, F., Dente, El, and Armon, M., *et al.*, Meteorological ingredients of heavy precipitation and subsequent lake filling episodes in the northwestern Sahara, EGUsphere [preprint], https://doi.org/10.5194/egusphere-2024-539, 2024.

The World Bank, Climate Change Knowledge Portal, 2024, on November 22, 2024

The World Bank, *Climate Risk Profile: Morocco*, (2021)

The World Bank, *Climate Variability, Drought, and Drought Management in Morocco's Agricultural Sector*, World Bank Group, (2018).

Tramblay, Y., Badi W., Driouech F., El S., Neppel L., and Servat E., Climate Change Impacts on ExtremePrecipitation in Morocco, *Global and Planetary Change*, 82-83: 104-114 (2012)

United States Geological Survey (USGS), Earthquake Hazards Program, on November

23, 2024 https://earthquake.usgs.gov/earthquakes/search

Vizy, E. K. and Cook, K. H. (2012), Mid-Twenty-First-Century Changes in Extreme Events over Northern and Tropical Africa, *Climate*, Vol.25, PP:5748-5767.

World Bank, (2022, July 20), https://www.worldbank.org/en/news/press-release/2022/07/20/moroccan-economy-slows-in-wake-of-drought-and-commodity-price-rises

Chapter 5

The PKO Activities of the Korean Medical Unit in MINURSO

Soonyoung Lee (Ret. Colonel)

Ret. Colonel, MSN. RN. Masters of Science in Nursing, Registered Nurse

✉ nurcaptain@gmail.com

She is a retired army colonel in the Republic of Korea and holds a Master of Science in Nursing. She graduated from the Korea Armed Forces Nursing Academy (KAFNA) and served as a nursing officer for 34 years. She lectured on nursing and served as the Chief of Teaching Division and the Director of the Military Nursing Research Institute at the KAFNA. Additionally, I worked as the Chief of Preventive Medicine at the Armed Forces Medical Command. After retirement, she has served as the Vice President of the Korean Coaching Association and the President of the Health Leaders Forum.

I. Introduction

South Korea's history of overseas military deployments spans 60 years as of 2024, beginning with its involvement in the Vietnam War in 1964. Since the Korean War, South Korea has transformed from a recipient of international aid into an economic powerhouse, actively participating in development assistance projects worldwide. Through these deployments, South Korea has cultivated an image as a peace-loving nation, enhanced its international reputation, and advanced its national prestige. Additionally, these efforts have significantly contributed to global peace and security while serving the nation's broader interests.

The objectives of South Korea's overseas deployments are multifaceted. First, they aim to repay the international community for the aid received during the Korean War, fulfilling a moral obligation. Second, they enhance South Korea's global standing by actively participating in peacekeeping missions and preparing for potential future assistance needs. Third, they fulfill the duties expected of a United Nations member state. Lastly, they contribute to the development of joint operational capabilities. Over the decades, South Korea's military has achieved these goals through its diverse overseas deployment activities.

Since its inception, the South Korean military has undertaken numerous overseas missions, including but not limited to the Republic of Korea Military Command in Vietnam, the Zaytun Division in Iraq, the Araw Unit for disaster recovery in the Philippines, and the Dan-bi Unit for reconstruction in Haiti. Other notable deployments include the Oshino Unit in Afghanistan, the medical support unit in Western Sahara in Morocco, and contributions to peacekeeping and reconstruction efforts in Somalia, Angola, East Timor, and Afghanistan. Currently, South Korean forces are active in missions such as the Dong-myeong Peacekeeping Unit in Lebanon, the Akh Training Unit in the UAE, the Han-bit Reconstruction Support Unit in South Sudan, and the Cheong-hae Anti-piracy Unit near Somalia.

Among these, the deployment of a medical unit to Western Sahara stands out as a particularly significant and enduring mission. Western Sahara, a desert region in southern Morocco 12,147 kilometers from South Korea, remains largely unfamiliar to most South Koreans, with minimal prior interaction between the two regions. In the wake of Spanish colonial rule, a territorial dispute in the region led to the establishment of MINURSO (United Nations Mission for the Referendum in Western Sahara) by UN Security Council Resolution 690 in 1991.

Responding to the UN's request, South Korea dispatched a military medical support unit to MINURSO in 1994, becoming the second contingent to join the mission.

The author of this paper was urgently deployed to Western Sahara in April 1995 as a replacement for a nursing officer who returned to South Korea due to health issues. Over the course of 11 months, the author adapted to the harsh climate, challenging terrain, and unique cultural environment of the MINURSO operational area. During this time, the author performed medical support duties, rotating between the central clinic and forward clinics at various team sites.

This paper draws upon the author's personal experiences and a thorough review of relevant reports, academic studies, and news articles. It explores the organization, operations, and achievements of the Korean Medical Support Unit's deployment to Western Sahara. By analyzing these aspects, the paper aims to propose recommendations for improving medical support operations and developing cooperative strategies in preparation for a stabilized regional environment.

II. The Korean Medical Unit's Deployment

1. The Background and Preparation for Deployment

On April 28, 1994, South Korea received a formal request from the United Nations to participate in the peacekeeping operation (PKO) in

Western Sahara. In response, a field survey team comprising six officials from the Ministry of Foreign Affairs and the Ministry of National Defense was dispatched between March 25 and April 2, 1994, to evaluate the local situation. Following the field assessment, the South Korean government confirmed the deployment through a Cabinet decision on May 30, 1994, and approval from the temporary National Assembly on July 14, 1994.

At the time, the Swiss Medical Support Unit had been serving in Western Sahara since September 1991. However, after a helicopter accident at a southern team site, the Swiss unit decided to discontinue its mission and requested approval from the UN to withdraw. This led to the transfer of the MINURSO medical support mission to South Korea's Medical Support Unit. The Swiss contingent withdrew on August 15, 1994.

South Korea's Ministry of National Defense established the Korean Military Medical Unit (KMU) on June 30, 1994, consisting of 42 personnel. Pre-deployment training was conducted at the Army Comprehensive Administrative School over three weeks to ensure mission readiness. This training included instruction on MINURSO's objectives, local conditions, cultural sensitivities, environmental challenges, and language skills. Starting with the fifth contingent, the training was extended to four weeks (188 hours), covering English language skills, PKO tasks, specialized medical skills, and briefings from experienced personnel.

2. The Operational Area

The operation area of MINURSO was situated in **Northwestern Africa** in southern Morocco, bordered by the **North Atlantic Ocean** to the northwest, **Algeria** to the east-northeast, and **Mauritania** to the east and south. The area was approximately **266,000 square kilometers** (according to the UN)

The region is primarily an **arid desert**, featuring **low, flat desert plains** along the western coastline and **small mountainous areas** in the east, where elevations reach up to **600 meters**. The interior experiences **extreme summer heat**, with average temperatures peaking at **43-45°C** during **July and August**, while winters remain **hot to very hot** during the day (25-30°C). However, nighttime temperatures can drop below **0°C** in the northern regions during **December and January**, occasionally resulting in freezing conditions.

The MINURSO operational area covers an extensive desert region, with its headquarters located in Laayoune, where the primary management and coordination of the UN peacekeeping mission take place. To conduct ceasefire monitoring and reconnaissance missions by UN forces across Western Sahara, MINURSO has divided its operational area into northern and southern regions, with headquarters and multiple team sites in each region.

During the time KMU conducted its mission locally, a total of 10 team sites were in operation within the area. In the northern region, there were five team sites: Smara, Mahbes, Mehaires, Tifariti, and Bir Lahlou, with the Northern Command Headquarters located in Smara, the key base in the northern region of the Moroccan Sahara.

In the southern region of the Moroccan Sahara, the team sites were located in Awsard, Dakhla, Mijek, Aguanit, and Umm Dreiga, while the Southern Command Headquarters was situated in the southern coastal city of Dakhla.

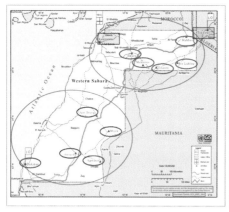 

Operational Area of Western Sahara (Left)   Team site (Right)

3. Operation of KMU

The KMU's first contingent arrived in Western Sahara on September 6, 1994, and established medical facilities in Laayoune southern Morocco on October 3. Additional forward clinics were set up in the northern and southern regions, and medical services expanded also to the Tindouf region, Algeria, during the second contingent's tenure.

Forward Medical Posts and Coverage

- **Northern Sector:** Located in Smara, this post supported team sites in Mahbas, Mhares, Tifariti, and Bir Lahlou. *(Morocco)*
- **Southern Sector:** Located in Awsard, this post supported team sites in Umm Dreiga, Mijek, Dakhla, and Aguanit. The Southern sector Command was located in Dakhla, but considering accessibility to each team site, a forward medical post for the southern sector was deployed in Awsard. *(Morocco)*
- **Tindouf Command:** A clinic was opened in this Polisario region to provide medical services. *(Algeria)*

Each post was staffed by one doctor and one nurse officer, who rotated every two weeks and conducted weekly medical visits to each team site. During rotations, ground transport was used for the Northern post, while rotary-wing aircraft was used for the Southern post, and fixed-wing aircraft was used for Tindouf.

Medical Mission of KMU

According to MINURSO's Standard Operating Procedures (SOP), the KMU's key responsibilities included:

- Providing Level 1 and 2 medical care to all MINURSO personnel, including emergency first aid and patient evacuation.

- Referring personnel to higher-level medical facilities when necessary.
- Operating two forward medical teams under the Level 1 care concept.
- Conducting preventive medical activities, such as sanitation checks and pest control.

Offering medical services to foreign diplomats and international personnel associated with MINURSO.

The KMU maintained Level 1, 2 capabilities during its deployment and the UN's Level 1 and Level 2 medical facility standards are as follows:

- **Level 1 Medical Facility:** Basic primary care facilities addressing minor injuries and illnesses.
- **Level 2 Medical Facility:** Advanced facilities equipped for emergency surgeries and serious conditions.

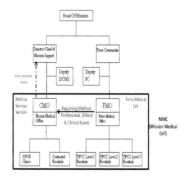

Category	Level I	Level II
Treament	immediate life-saving and resuscitation capabilities along with routine clinical care.	damage control surgery, post-operative services, intensive care-resuscitation. in-patient services, record maintenance and administrative support.
Staffing	2 medical officers 6 paramedics or nurses 3 support staffs including an ambulance driver	57 or 67
Capability	20 outpatients per day Temporary holding capacity of 5 patients for upto 2 days Hold medical supplies and consumables for 60 days	3 to 4 surgeries per day 10-20 inpatient for upto 7 days 40 outpatients per day 10 dental consultations per day Hold medical supplies and consumables for 60 days

The UN's Level 1 and Level 2
medical facility standards

Integrated Mission Medical
Support Structure

Organizational Structure of KMU

The KMU provided Level 2 medical services to UN personnel, including UN Military Observers (UNMO), CIVPOL (UN civilian police), and other UN civilian staff. Additionally, it offered public and emergency medical services to local residents. Initially, the KMU consisted of 42 personnel, including 8 doctors and 6 nurses. However, starting with the fifth contingent, the unit was reduced to 20 personnel to align with MINURSO's scaled-down operations.

The senior medical officer in KMO managed medical operations, collaborated with the Field Medical Officer (FMO), and ensured proper documentation and reporting to UN headquarters. Key duties also included training personnel, coordinating evacuations, and overseeing medical supply logistics.

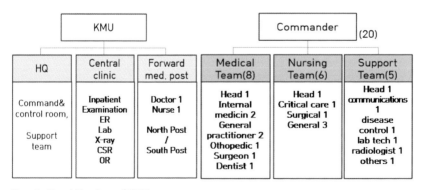

Oganizational Structure of KMU

4. Operational Activities and Achievements of KMU

The medical support mission of MINURSO provided Level 1 and Level 2 medical services to all personnel, and assisted in evacuating patients to higher-level medical facilities when necessary. The outcomes of this medical support mission can be summarized as follows:

- **Medical Support Statistics:** An analysis of the medical support data reveals that out of 58,888 patients treated, the most common conditions were internal medicine (32%), orthopedics (17%), dentistry (13%), and dermatology (10%). Among internal medicine cases, the most common conditions included upper respiratory tract diseases and headaches. Due to the nature of the mission, many UN Military Observers (UNMOs) experienced joint pain, including shoulder, back, knee, wrist, and ankle pain, leading to high demand for physical therapy. Additionally, internal medicine cases exhibited seasonal variation, with an increase in cases during the winter months.

- **Emergency Evacuations** (CASEVAC): Data from the seven-year period between 1999 and 2006 shows a total of 36 emergency evacuations. The primary causes of injury were traffic accidents (11 cases), mission-related injuries (10 cases, including a mine explosion), and medical conditions. Specific conditions included fractures (11), angina or myocardial infarction (5), multiple injuries (4), lacerations (4), strokes (3), and other issues such as pneumonia, asthma, mine explosion injuries, unknown causes of fever, and suicide. Notably, nine emergency evacuations were conducted from team sites located outside the urban areas of Laayoune and Dakhla in Southern Morocco and Tindouf in West Algeria.

- **Preventive Medical Activities:** The underdeveloped sanitation environment of the region coupled with extreme temperature fluctuations and harsh natural conditions, such as sandstorms, posed significant health risks to personnel. To mitigate these risks, regular sanitation checks and pest control measures were conducted at the command post and all team sites. The results of these checks were reported to the military commander and used to inform future planning. Efforts to enhance food and water inspections were strengthened, and hygiene education at team sites was prioritized to improve overall sanitary conditions. Notably, in the Tindouf settlement area, pest control and hygiene checks were successfully carried out, leading to significant improvements.
- **Medical Record Management:** The management of outpatient and inpatient visits, as well as pharmaceutical and equipment inventories, which had previously been handled manually, was digitized using Excel-based statistical programs. This transition greatly improved the efficiency of the medical support unit's operations and provided crucial data for peacekeeping operations (PKO), which was also used for statistical research purposes.

The KMU was deployed on August 9, 1994, with the first contingent taking over the mission from the Swiss military. Over the course of 12 years, a total of 542 personnel served in the KMU, successfully fulfilling their duties. The unit concluded its mission on May 13, 2006, following a handover ceremony with the Malaysian military. This deployment marked a historic achievement, becoming the longest overseas military deployment in South Korea's history, spanning over 60 years. The KMU received widespread praise for its humanitarian assistance to the local population and for ensuring stable conditions for MINURSO personnel. In fact, during the withdrawal of the 23rd contingent in 2006, the MINURSO Special Representative commended the KMU, stating:

"The high medical skills and diligent support of the KMU left a lasting impression on all UN personnel. I deeply appreciate that the 23rd contingent treated over 58,000 people and made significant contributions to UN activities."

Furthermore, the MINURSO Force Commander remarked:

"I highly commend the KMU's mission execution and was particularly impressed by their proactive approach as soldiers."

Medical treatment for UN personnel at the central clinic in Laayoune.

First aid training at the team sites

MINURSO Medical Unit Handover Ceremony (Republic of Korea – Malaysia) on May 13 2006

III. Challenges and limitations

During the author's 11-month mission in the MINURSO operational area in Western Sahara, a range of challenges were encountered due to the local geographical, climatic, cultural, and economic factors. In addition, the author has summarized the challenges faced by the Korean Medical Unit (KMU) during their peacekeeping mission based on return reports and other literature sources. These challenges include:

- **Harsh Climate:** The extreme heat and frequent sandstorms in the region led to frequent equipment failures, as well as difficulties in field deployment and patient transport. The hot desert climate made outdoor physical activities difficult during the day, and emergency equipment that needed to be operated outdoors often faced functional issues. Moreover, some medical supplies could not be stored properly due to the lack of cooling facilities. Sandstorms also created significant operational challenges, as sand dust would accumulate inside hospital facilities and cause malfunctions in sensitive medical equipment. To mitigate these issues, efforts were made to maintain a stable environment for equipment and medication storage, and medical support plans, including evacuation strategies, were tailored to the climate.
- **Vast Desert Terrain:** The expansive desert landscape made it challenging to provide timely medical support and transport medical supplies. The distance between the central clinic and team sites often stretched over several hundred kilometers, with personnel and supplies primarily transported via regular flights. In emergency situations, such as

scorpion or snake bites, it was often impossible to replenish vaccines for immediate use. To overcome these challenges, it would be beneficial to explore alternative transportation options, such as drones, which could bypass terrain limitations.

- **Water Quality Issues:** The local water, with its high salinity or insufficient purification, posed problems for operating certain medical equipment. Bottled water was used for sterilization and laboratory examination equipment. Introducing advanced water purification technologies from Korea could help ensure a reliable and safe water supply for medical operations.

- **Language Barriers:** A lack of proficiency in French and Arabic made communication with local populations and the provision of medical treatment more difficult. It is crucial that pre-deployment training includes language courses, enabling personnel to acquire the language skills necessary for effective communication and medical service delivery.

- **Manual Medical Record System:** The absence of an automated medical record system hindered the efficiency and consistency of medical tasks, such as vaccinations and tracking test results. The KMU used a separate medical record form, which was incompatible with MINURSO's forms, leading to operational inefficiencies. While Excel was used to compile patient statistics, there is a need for more advanced, automated systems to enhance operational efficiency and standardization.

- **Challenges of Frequent Air Travel:** Frequent air travel for team site rotations and medical rounds posed challenges, especially for individuals suffering from motion sickness. Concerns about the risk of accidents also arose. To alleviate the burden of frequent air and ground transport, adopting telemedicine systems, such as those currently used by the Republic of Korea Armed Forces for personnel in remote areas, and utilizing drones for medical supply deliveries would be beneficial.

· **Limited Communication Tools:** The absence of advanced communication tools, such as cell phones and the internet, created significant difficulties in communication between team sites and headquarters. As noted by Lee et al. *(2005)*, deployed military personnel often face low family functioning and social support due to communication restrictions. This can lead to psychological challenges. Proactive measures and thorough pre-deployment reviews should address these concerns and enhance the mental well-being of personnel.

• **Limited Conveniences:** The lack of certain comforts, such as hair salons, contributed to a lower quality of life for personnel during the deployment.

IV. Recommendations for future collaborations

The current situation in Western Sahara remains unresolved. However, the international community, including the United Nations, continues to work toward a resolution. In anticipation of a future resolution and stabilization, the following collaboration strategies are proposed based on the experiences of the KMU during its deployment.

• Expansion of Medical Field Exchanges
  – Share information and host academic seminars on locally prevalent diseases *(such as climate-related illnesses and endemic diseases)* and trauma cases.
  – Promote joint research projects on common health issues in the

Sahara region.

- Provide educational and training programs (both online and offline) and facilitate the exchange of qualified faculty members.

• Collaboration on Testing and Commercializing Korean Medical Technologies for Desert Environments

- Develop and deploy medical equipment and facilities suited to desert terrains.

- Introduce evacuation equipment, such as ambulances and medical air transport helicopters.

- Explore the use of drone technology to transport medical supplies efficiently.

- Develop a power supply system that can ensure the continuous use of medical equipment and provide uninterrupted medical care.

• Support for Improving Medical Infrastructure.

- Assist in modernizing healthcare facilities using Korean technology and systems. This could include health clinic modernization projects similar to those previously carried out in collaboration with the World Health Organization (WHO) in various African countries.

• Transfer of Successful Korean Military Medical System.

- Implement medical air evacuation control systems.

- Establish infectious disease surveillance systems.

- Develop simulation-based training programs.

- Utilize telemedicine systems to enhance medical support in remote areas.

V. Conclusion

The Republic of Korea Medical Support Unit's 12-year deployment to Western Sahara in southern Morocco as part of MINURSO is not only the longest deployment in South Korea's military history, but it also stands as a testament to the Korean military's ability to provide medical services that meet the United Nations' standards. Despite the extended deployment period, the United Nations consistently requested the continued contribution of the Korean Medical Unit, reflecting the positive evaluation of the unit's medical services by MINURSO personnel.

During the 12 years of service, 542 personnel from 23 rotations provided medical care to 58,880 patients, supported 36 emergency evacuations, managed environmental sanitation, and conducted preventive health activities, including vaccinations and health checks for both UN personnel and local residents.

Through these efforts, the Korean military gained invaluable expertise in medical operations in desert environments, leading to heightened interest in medical and evacuation technologies. This accumulated experience will serve as a driving force for future collaborative initiatives in the Sahara region.

■ References

Encyclopædia Britannica. *Western Sahara Summary.*

Kim, HS. (2006). A Research on PKO (Peace Keeping Operation) for Korean Medical Supporting Force – Focusing on Activities in Western Sahara. *Military Nursing Research,* 24*(2).*

Kim, SH(2022). The need of roles of MINURSO and military observer. Peace Keeping Operations, Vol 25.

Korea Joint Staff Command. (2006, May 16). The Activity Report of Western Sahara Korea Medical Unit. New Release.

Lee, J.-Y. (2009). A Study on Overseas-Dispatched Soldiers' Stress Reactions and Stress Factors as Compared with Those of Mother Corps Soldiers. *Military Nursing Research,* 27(2).

Lee, Y.-M., Park, D.-E., Kwon, M.-O., Yang, J.-I., Ann, E.-G., & Ji, J.-E. (2005). Factors Influencing Functional Status in Soldiers of Troops Dispatched Overseas. *Military Medical Research,* 41(1), 39-50.

Lee, Y. (2008). Retrospect and Prospects of Overseas Deployments of the Korean Military. *Military Research,* 125, 79-1

United Nations Department of Peacekeeping Operations & Department of Field Support. (2015). *Medical Support Manual for United Nations Field Missions* (3rd ed.).

United Nations Mission for the Referendum in Western Sahara (MINURSO). (n.d.). *Chronology of Events.* Retrieved from https://minurso.unmissions.org/ chronology-events

United Nations Security Council. (1991). *Resolution 690.*

United Nations Security Council. (2024). Situation Concerning Western Sahara, Report of the Secretary-General.

United Nations. (1999). *Medical Support Manual for United Nations Peacekeeping*

Operations (2nd ed.).

Yonhap News Agency. (2005, June 1). [Online article]. Retrieved from https://www.yna. co.kr/view/IIS20050601003500999?page=1

Chapter 6

The Neuroscientific Mechanisms of Empathy and Peace Consciousness and Some Implications for Morocco and Korea's Educational Cooperation

Hyoungbin Park (Seoul National University of Education)

✉ profphb@snue.ac.kr

She is a professor in the Department of Ethics Education at Seoul National University of Education (SNUE) in Seoul, Republic of Korea. As an accomplished author, she has written several works, including The Moral Intelligence Lesson (in Korean), AI Ethics, Neuroscience, and Education (in Korean), Theory and Practice of Moral Pedagogy (in Korean), the series If You Had to Choose, What Would You Do? (in Korean), Neuroscience and Moral Education (in Korean), Artificial Intelligence Ethics and Moral Education (in Korean), AI Era Transforming Education in Korea (in Korean), among others. Currently, she serves as the Chief of the SNUE Neuroethics Convergence Education Research Center (NCERC) and also as the Chief of the SNUE Value Ethics AI Hub Center (VEAHC). Her ongoing research interests span across Moral Psychology, Neuroethics, Reunification Education, Citizenship Education, and the Diagnosi of Morality.

I. Introduction

In a world increasingly defined by global conflicts and social divisions, understanding the neurobiological foundations of empathy and peace consciousness has become imperative. These concepts are vital for fostering compassion, mutual understanding, and peaceful coexistence. Although traditionally explored in psychology, philosophy, and the social sciences, recent advancements in neuroscience provide novel insights into their biological basis.

This paper aims to synthesize current neuroscientific research on empathy and peace consciousness by presenting a multidisciplinary framework that examines how the brain enables these capacities. By investigating neural correlates such as the mirror neuron system, the limbic system, and the prefrontal cortex, this study seeks to offer a deeper understanding of the brain mechanisms underlying empathy and the cultivation of peace consciousness. Additionally, the conclusion aims to propose educational cooperative strategies between Korea and Morocco based on the insights gained from this discussion.

II. Theoretical Foundations

1. Empathy: Definitions and Theoretical Perspectives

One of the interpersonal faculties that support and promote everyday social interactions is empathy, the ability to share and understand others' affective states (Tousignant et al., 2017). Empathy is a multifaceted construct that plays a crucial role in human social interactions and relationships. It is generally defined as the ability to understand and share the feelings of others. However, empathy encompasses a range of components and has been conceptualized in various ways across different theoretical frameworks.

The term 'empathy' was coined over 100 years ago by Titchener, an adaptation of the German word Einfühlung. According to Stotland and colleagues, discussions of empathy may even date back to "the beginnings of philosophical thought". Despite this extensive history, empathy is not a well-defined notion. Instead, there are perhaps as many definitions as there are authors in the field (Cuff et al., 2016). Titchener first coined the term empathy in the early 1900s as an English translation of the German term Einfühlung (Lishner et al., 2020).

Affective Empathy refers to the capacity to respond with an appropriate emotion to another's mental states (Thompson, N. M., Van Reekum, C. M., & Chakrabarti, B., 2022). It involves emotional contagion, where an individual experiences emotion that are congruent with another person's emotional state. This form of empathy allows individuals to emotionally resonate with others, facilitating deeper emotional connections. Second, Cognitive Empathy, also known as perspective-taking, involves the ability to understand another person's thoughts and feelings (Dorris et al, 2022). It requires a more deliberate and conscious effort to comprehend another's perspective, enabling individuals to intellectually grasp what others are experiencing. Third, Compassionate Empathy, sometimes called empathic concern, goes beyond merely understanding and feeling another's emotions. It also includes the motivation to help or support the person in need. Empathy is understanding another's world affectively and emotionally, while compassion uses this understanding to improve others' lives. Compassion fulfills our needs to survive, connect, and find mates (Goldstein et al, 2021). Engaging in empathic communication can enrich relationships, allowing children to nurture this instinct and connect meaningfully with others. This form of empathy is crucial in driving prosocial behaviors and fostering supportive social environments.

First, from an Evolutionary Perspective, empathy is considered an adaptive trait that has evolved to facilitate social bonding and cooperation among humans. One likely source of empathetic responses in mammals stems from the phylogenetically ancient practice of caring for their offspring (Decety, J., Norman, G. J., Berntson, G. G., & Cacioppo, J. T.,

2012). It enhances group cohesion and survival by promoting prosocial behaviors, which are essential for the well-being of social groups. Second, the Developmental research brings an interesting perspective on how the different components of empathy interact with each other and emerge at different paces, and how their alteration during early years can affect social abilities (Tousignant, B., Eugène, F., & Jackson, P. L., 2017). From early childhood, individuals learn to recognize and interpret emotional cues, gradually refining their empathic abilities. This perspective highlights the dynamic nature of empathy as it matures across the lifespan. Third, the Neuroscientific Perspective draws on recent advances in neuroscience to identify specific brain regions associated with empathy. Key areas such as the mirror neuron system, the anterior insula, and the anterior cingulate cortex are involved in processing both the emotional and cognitive aspects of empathy (Zebarjadi, 2024). These findings provide a biological basis for understanding how empathy functions at a neural level. Finally, the Social and Cultural Perspectives emphasize that empathy is shaped by social norms and cultural contexts (Jami et al, 2024). Different societies may prioritize various aspects of empathy, influencing how it is expressed and valued. This perspective acknowledges that empathy is not only a personal trait but also a socially constructed and culturally mediated phenomenon.

Understanding the diverse definitions and theoretical perspectives of empathy is essential for exploring its role in promoting peace consciousness and fostering harmonious social interactions. This multifaceted approach allows researchers to examine empathy from various angles, contributing to a more comprehensive understanding of its mechanisms and implications.

2. Peace Consciousness: Conceptual Frameworks

Peace is a state of calm and nonviolence that exists both internally and externally. Inner peace is the key to achieving external peace. Due to anger, stress, unhappiness, and various other factors, individuals who claim to be peaceful may exhibit severely violent traits, attitudes, and behaviors. This is often a result of a lack of internal peace (Esho, 2024). Peace consciousness can be broadly defined as the awareness and intentional cultivation of peaceful thoughts, attitudes, and behaviors at both individual and collective levels. It involves two primary dimensions.

Inner Peace refers to a state of mental and emotional calmness and harmony within oneself. It is characterized by self-awareness, emotional regulation, and a profound sense of contentment and tranquility, often achieved through practices such as mindfulness and meditation (Liu et al, 2015). Outer Peace focuses on actively promoting harmonious relationships and nonviolent conflict resolution in interpersonal and societal contexts (Bevington, 2018). It involves applying peaceful principles in social interactions, conflict resolution, and the promotion of justice and equity within society.

Various theoretical frameworks have been developed to understand

and cultivate peace consciousness, each offering unique insights into how peace can be achieved and sustained. First, the Positive Peace Theory developed by Johan Galtung distinguishes between negative peace, which is the absence of violence, and positive peace, which is the presence of social justice and harmony (Mukerji, S., 2021). Galtung's framework emphasizes that true peace involves more than just ending conflict; it requires the proactive creation of systems that promote equity, justice, and positive relationships within societies. Second, the Peace education attempts to help students move away from a position of fear and apathy to a condition of becoming and staying engaged with others. Peace educators address the root causes of conflict and violence. The long term goal is to create in human conscious- ness the continued desire to pursue peaceful solutions to problems of violence and to transform human values toward nonviolence (Morrison, 2015). This approach aims to develop critical thinking, conflict resolution skills, and global awareness, enabling individuals to contribute to a culture of peace. Third, the Mindfulness and Peace Consciousness framework, drawing from Buddhist and other contemplative traditions, proposes that cultivating present-moment awareness through mindfulness can lead to more peaceful states of mind and behavior (Brantmeier, 2007). Fourth, the Salutogenesis and Peace approach suggests that fostering a strong sense of meaning and connection in life contributes to peace at both the personal and societal levels (Daniel & Ottemöller, 2022). Fifth, the Cultural Peace Framework examines how cultural values, beliefs, and practices influence the development of peace consciousness. Intercultural peace (IP) is a peaceful means of promoting multiculturalism or interculturalism because IP is required for peaceful coexistence in the face of diversity; it teaches respect and tolerance. When the five families of peace are considered. peace as a holistic peace that embraces all aspects of human nature. It is not only rational, but also emotional, mental and spiritual. Human encounters, relationships, communication styles and behaviors are all addressed (Esho, 2024). This framework recognizes the diversity of peace concepts across different societies and highlights the role of cultural narratives and traditions in shaping attitudes toward peace.

These conceptual frameworks collectively highlight the multifaceted nature of peace consciousness, encompassing individual psychological states, interpersonal dynamics, and broader societal structures. They underscore that peace consciousness is not merely the absence of conflict but an active, dynamic state that can be cultivated and expanded through various means.

III. Neuroscientific Foundations of Empathy

1. Role of Mirror Neurons in Empathy

The discovery of mirror neurons has significantly advanced our understanding of the neural mechanisms underlying empathy. These specialized brain cells play a crucial role in our ability to understand and share the experiences of others.

Mirror neurons are primarily located in the premotor cortex and the inferior parietal lobule. Mirror neurons, the recently discovered mechanism underlying empathy, are characterized, followed by a theory of brain-to-brain coupling. This neuro-tuning, seen as a kind of synchronization (SYNC) between brains and between individuals, takes various forms, including frequency aspects of language use and the understanding that develops regardless of the difference in spoken tongues (Praszkier, 2016). They fire both when an animal performs a specific action and when it observes the same action being performed by another, providing a neural basis for understanding others' actions and intentions.

The role of mirror neurons in emotional empathy is significant. The development of newer neurophysiological assessment tools and the concept of the whole-brain network has shed more light on its neurological basis and how it shapes our social adaptations. Contrary to the existing notion of cortical areas controlling specific tasks and limbic system controlling emotions, the role of shared networks, allostatic-interoceptive systems operating on multimodal predictions, mirror neurons, and specific neurotransmitters in empathy is quite evident. The salience network is one such non-specific neural network that connects the brain areas primarily responsible for empathy, namely the cingulate cortex, insular cortex, and part of the thalamus, hypothalamus, amygdala, substantia nigra, ventral tegmental area, and ventral striatum.

The meticulously crafted mirror neuron system also modulates empathy as it determines the imitation capability. Marked changes in empathy are seen in conditions like schizophrenia, major depressive disorders, bipolar disorder, and dementia. It is implicated in learning, development of social skills, mutual trust and compassion, improved workplace environment, performance, and personal relations, and promoting positive lifestyle and happiness. A substantial level of deep empathy and social relationships contribute to happiness and vice-versa (Sahu, 2023).

Beyond understanding actions and emotions, mirror neurons contribute to social cognition by enabling perspective-taking and the understanding of others' mental states. They facilitate emotional contagion, aid in recognizing facial expressions, and contribute to pain empathy by activating similar neural circuits involved in first-hand pain experiences. The discovery of mirror neurons has lent strong support to simulation theories of empathy, suggesting that we understand others by internally simulating their experiences. This aligns with the concept of embodied cognition, where our understanding of others is deeply grounded in our own sensorimotor experiences. it is important to recognize that empathy is a complex phenomenon involving multiple neural networks. Continued research in this area is essential for deepening our comprehension of empathy and for exploring its implications in social behaviors and disorders characterized by empathic deficits.

2. Limbic System and Emotional Processing in Empathic Responses

The limbic system, a network of interconnected brain structures, is central to emotional processing and crucial for empathy. It includes key areas such as the amygdala, hippocampus, anterior cingulate cortex (ACC), insula, and hypothalamus, which work together to mediate emotional experiences and influence how we empathize.

First, the amygdala plays a critical role in detecting and processing emotional stimuli, particularly negative emotions like fear and anger (Wang et al., 2023). It helps us recognize and respond to others' emotional states, laying the groundwork for empathy. Second, the hippocampus, while mainly involved in memory, also links past emotional experiences with present observations, enhancing our ability to empathize (Qasim et al., 2023). The amygdala and insula contribute to emotional recognition and resonance, while the ACC integrates emotional experiences with cognitive processes. Third, the insula is involved in emotional awareness and plays a key role in empathy by processing bodily sensations linked to emotions (Lotze, 2024). It also supports embodied simulation, helping us internally mimic others' emotional states. Fourth, the limbic system works closely with the prefrontal cortex to regulate empathic responses (Shepelenko & Kosonogov, 2023). The prefrontal cortex modulates limbic activity, ensuring our emotional reactions are balanced and appropriate, preventing overwhelming emotional contagion. Fifth, individual differences in empathy reflect neural plasticity, with variations in limbic structure and function correlating with empathic abilities (Valk et al., 2023). The limbic system's plasticity suggests that empathic capacities can be developed through experience and training.

Overall, the limbic system is essential for the recognition, resonance, and regulation of emotions fundamental to empathy, interacting with other brain regions to ensure our responses are balanced and socially constructive.

IV. Neuroscientific Mechanisms of Peace Consciousness

1. Neural Networks Associated with Peace Consciousness: The Default Mode Network

The discovery of the default mode network (DMN) has fundamentally transformed our understanding of human brain function. The DMN is a collection of distributed and interconnected brain regions that are typically suppressed when an individual is focused on external stimuli; however, in the absence of attention to external stimuli, the DMN switches or 'defaults' to internally focused thought processes, such as self-reflection, daydreaming, mind wandering, recall of per- sonal experiences, and envisioning the future. The Default Mode Network (DMN) is a network of brain regions that is most active when the brain is at rest and not focused on the external environment (Menon, 2023).

The finding of reduced gray matter in reward-related subcortical regions in high accepters is in line with previous findings that reported less susceptibility to extrinsic incentive in expert meditators compared to non-meditators, reflecting a sort of 'inner peace' state in meditators. Also, the right insula and the anterior cingulate cortex (dACC) may contribute to the achievement of this 'let it be' attitude toward internal arousing representations. These areas are key nodes of the salience network, which integrates internal and external information to guide behavior. The salience network is responsible for switching between the DMN and the central executive network, signalling the DMN to reduce its activity when attention is shifted from internal to external focus. Taken together, these results account for a difference between high accepters and low accepters in the management of internally generated arousing contents (Grecucci et al., 2023).

It plays a significant role in self-referential thinking, daydreaming, and the processing of emotions, making it a key player in the development and maintenance of peace consciousness. The DMN includes several key brain regions, such as the medial prefrontal cortex (mPFC), posterior cingulate cortex (PCC), precuneus, and angular gyrus. These regions are involved in introspection, reflection, and the integration of emotional and cognitive processes. (Brandmeyer & Delorme, 2021). When individuals engage in activities that promote peace consciousness, such as meditation or mindfulness practices, the DMN is often activated, facilitating a state of calm and self-awareness.

The DMN is deeply involved in the processing of moral and ethical considerations, which are essential for peace consciousness (Yonus, 2023). This network helps individuals reflect on their values, beliefs, and the impact of their actions on others, promoting empathy and understanding. Moreover, the DMN's role in social cognition is critical for peace consciousness. It enables individuals to simulate and predict the thoughts and feelings of others, which is essential for empathy and conflict resolution.

Alterations in DMN activity have been associated with various mental health conditions, such as depression and anxiety, which can impede peace consciousness. Interventions that target the DMN, such as mindfulness-based therapies, have been shown to enhance emotional regulation and reduce symptoms of these conditions (Broyd et al., 2009). The DMN's interaction with other neural networks, such as the salience network and the executive control network, is crucial for maintaining a balance between internal and external focus. This dynamic interaction is essential for applying the reflective insights gained from DMN activity to real-world situations, thereby enhancing the practical expression of peace consciousness. The Default Mode Network plays a pivotal role in the neural mechanisms underlying peace consciousness. By supporting introspection, moral reasoning, and social cognition, the DMN contributes to the cultivation of a mindset that values empathy, understanding, and peace. Understanding the DMN's function offers valuable insights into how individuals and societies can foster peace consciousness, ultimately contributing to a more compassionate and just world.

2. The Role of the Anterior Cingulate Cortex in Promoting Harmony and Non-Violence

The anterior cingulate cortex (ACC) is a vital brain region involved in cognitive and emotional processes essential for promoting harmony and non-violence, including emotional regulation, decision-making, impulse control, and social cognition (Agarwal et al., 2018).

First, the ACC is crucial for conflict monitoring, allowing individuals to detect and adjust behaviors to maintain harmonious relationships (Botvinick et al., 2001). It plays a key role in emotional regulation, helping manage emotional responses, which is important for responding to conflicts with calmness rather than aggression. Second, the ACC enhances empathy and impulse control, both of which are critical for non-violent behavior (Decety & Holvoet, 2021). Higher ACC activity is associated with greater empathy and better emotional regulation, supporting peaceful conflict resolution and increased compassion. Third, the ACC's neuroplasticity suggests that its capacity for promoting harmony can be enhanced through mindfulness and cognitive-behavioral therapies, potentially leading to more peaceful attitudes and behaviors (Tang & Tang, 2017).

Overall, the ACC is integral to fostering peace consciousness by supporting conflict monitoring, emotional regulation, and empathy. Understanding its functions offers valuable insights into promoting non-violence at both individual and societal levels.

V. Conclusion: Possibilities for Educational Cooperation between Korea and Morocco

In this paper, I explored the neuroscientific mechanisms underlying empathy and peace consciousness, emphasizing their roles in fostering harmonious social interactions and non-violent behavior. I examined key neural components, including the mirror neuron system, the limbic system, the Default Mode Network (DMN), and the anterior cingulate cortex (ACC). The mirror neuron system was identified as a fundamental neural substrate for empathy, enabling individuals to understand the emotions and intentions of others. The limbic system's role in emotional processing was emphasized, particularly its involvement in recognizing and regulating emotional responses.

The Default Mode Network was highlighted for its contribution to peace consciousness by supporting introspection, moral reasoning, and social cognition. The anterior cingulate cortex was discussed as a pivotal region in promoting harmony and non-violence, with roles in emotional regulation, decision-making, and impulse control. The interplay between these neural networks underscores the complexity of empathy and peace consciousness as multifaceted constructs. The findings suggest that these capacities emerge from dynamic interactions between multiple neural systems. The neuroscientific insights presented offer valuable perspectives on how empathy and peace consciousness can be nurtured and enhanced. Understanding the neural underpinnings provides a foundation for developing more effective interventions and educational programs aimed at promoting empathy and fostering a culture of peace.

The proposed collaboration initiatives aim to foster effective partnerships and enhance mutual goals. First, Korea and Morocco can co-develop educational programs that incorporate empathy-building and peace consciousness as core components. These programs can draw upon neuroscience-based approaches, such as mindfulness training, social-emotional learning, and conflict resolution strategies. Second, Teacher Training Programs: Exchange programs for educators can be established to share best practices in promoting empathy and peace consciousness in classrooms. Korean and Moroccan teachers can collaborate on integrating neuroscientific insights into lesson plans and teaching methods. Third, Student Exchange and Cultural Immersion Programs: By fostering intercultural understanding, student exchange programs can provide opportunities for Korean and Moroccan students to practice empathy and gain perspectives on peacebuilding in different cultural contexts. Fourth, Joint Research and Knowledge Sharing: Universities and research institutions in Korea and Morocco can collaborate on studies focusing on empathy and peace consciousness. This partnership can also support the creation of resources and tools for educators in both nations. Through these initiatives, Korea and Morocco can deepen their educational collaboration, enrich learning environments, and foster a shared commitment to empathy, peace consciousness, and global citizenship.

Future research should explore how these insights can be applied to real-world conflict resolution and peace-building programs. Additionally, studies on cultural differences affecting the neurological basis of peace consciousness are needed. The neuroscientific understanding of empathy and peace consciousness opens new possibilities for creating a more peaceful world, with wide-ranging applications from cultivating inner peace in individuals to resolving global conflicts.

■ References

Agarwal, S., Kumar, V., Agarwal, S., Brugnoli, M. P., & Agarwal, A. Meditational spiritual intercession and recovery from disease in palliative care: a literature review. *Annals of palliative medicine*, 7(1), 412-462. (2018).

Bevington, T., & Gregory, A. Restorative practice as peace practice. *Getting more out of restorative practice in schools: Practical approaches to improve school wellbeing and strengthen community engagement*, 189-201. (2018).

Botvinick, M. M., Braver, T. S., Barch, D. M., Carter, C. S., & Cohen, J. D. Conflict monitoring and cognitive control. *Psychological review*, 108(3), 624. (2001).

Brandmeyer, T., & Delorme, A. Meditation and the wandering mind: A theoretical framework of underlying neurocognitive mechanisms. *Perspectives on Psychological Science*, 16(1), 39-66. (2021).

Brantmeier, E. Connecting inner and outer peace: Buddhist meditation integrated with peace education. In Factis Pax: *Journal of Peace Education and Social Justice*, 1(2). (2007)

Broyd, S. J., Demanuele, C., Debener, S., Helps, S. K., James, C. J., & Sonuga-Barke, E. J. Default-mode brain dysfunction in mental disorders: a systematic review. *Neuroscience & biobehavioral reviews*, 33. (2009).

Cuff, B. M., Brown, S. J., Taylor, L., & Howat, D. J. Empathy: A review of the concept. *Emotion review*, 8(2), 144-153. (2016).

Daniel, M., & Ottemöller, F. P. G. Salutogenesis and migration. *The*

Decety, J., & Holvoet, C. The emergence of empathy: A developmental neuroscience perspective. *Developmental Review*, 62, 100999. (2021).

Decety, J., Norman, G. J., Berntson, G. G., & Cacioppo, J. T. (2012). A neurobehavioral evolutionary perspective on the mechanisms underlying empathy. Progress in neurobiology, 98(1), 38-48.

Dorris, L., Young, D., Barlow, J., Byrne, K., & Hoyle, R. Cognitive empathy across the lifespan. *Developmental Medicine & Child Neurology*, 64(12), 1524-1531. (2022).

Esho, E. O. The paradigm of peace enhancing peace culture. Journal of Aggression, *Conflict and Peace Research*, 16(1), 83-97. (2024).

Goldstein, S., Brooks, R. B., Goldstein, S., & Brooks, R. B. Compassionate empathy. *Tenacity in children: Nurturing the seven instincts for lifetime success*, 57-70. (2021).

Grecucci, A., Ghomroudi, P. A., Monachesi, B., & Messina, I. The neural signature of inner peace: morphometric differences between high and low accepters. arXiv preprint arXiv:2310.13318. (2023).

handbook of salutogenesis, 503-511. (2022).

Jami, P. Y., Walker, D. I., & Mansouri, B. Interaction of empathy and culture: a review.

Current Psychology, 43(4), 2965-2980. (2024).

Lishner, D. A., Stocks, E. L., & Steinert, S. W. Empathy. Encyclopedia of personality and individual differences, 1352-1359. (2020).

Liu, X., Xu, W., Wang, Y., Williams, J. M. G., Geng, Y., Zhang, Q., & Liu, X. Can inner peace be improved by mindfulness training: a randomized controlled trial. *Stress and Health*, 31(3), 245-254. (2015).

Lotze, M. (2024). Emotional processing impairments in patients with insula lesions following stroke. *NeuroImage, 120591.Menon, V. 20 years of the default mode network: A review and synthesis. Neuron*, 111(16), 2469-2487. (2023).

Morrison, M. L. Peacelearning and Its Relationship to the Teaching of Nonviolence. *Democracy & Education*, 23(1). (2015).

Mukerji, S. From negative to positive peace: Meeting of two seminal minds. environment and society, 3(3). (2021).

Praszkier, R. Empathy, mirror neurons and SYNC. *Mind & Society*, 15, 1-25. (2016).

Qasim, S. E., Mohan, U. R., Stein, J. M., & Jacobs, J. Neuronal activity in the human amygdala and hippocampus enhances emotional memory encoding. *Nature Human Behaviour*, 7(5), 754-764. (2023).

Sahu, S. Experiencing others: The science of empathy. In *Understanding happiness: An explorative view* (pp. 249-264). Singapore: Springer Nature Singapore. (2023).

Shepelenko, A. Y., & Kosonogov, V. V. Cerebral Support for Making Donation-Related Decision with Altruistic and Egoistic Motives. *Neuroscience and Behavioral Physiology*, 53(2), 242-246. (2023).

Tang, Y. Y., & Tang, Y. Y. Brain Mechanisms of Mindfulness Meditation. *The Neuroscience of Mindfulness Meditation: How the Body and Mind Work Together to Change Our Behaviour*, 9-22. (2017).

Thompson, N. M., Van Reekum, C. M., & Chakrabarti, B. Cognitive and affective empathy relate differentially to emotion regulation. *Affective Science*, 3(1), 118-134. (2022).

Tousignant, B., Eugène, F., & Jackson, P. L. A developmental perspective on the neural bases of human empathy. *Infant Behavior and Development*, 48, 5-12. (2017).

Valk, S. L., Kanske, P., Park, B. Y., Hong, S. J., Böckler, A., Trautwein, F. M., & Singer, T. Functional and microstructural plasticity following social and interoceptive mental training. *Elife*, 12, e85188. (2023).

Wang, Y., Luo, L., Chen, G., Luan, G., Wang, X., Wang, Q., & Fang, F. Rapid processing of invisible fearful faces in the human amygdala. *Journal of Neuroscience*, 43(8), 1405-1413. (2023).

Yonus, R. Ethical Limbo and Enhanced Informed Consent in Psychedelic-Assisted Therapy: Identifying New Challenges and Ethical Dimensions. (2023).

Zebarjadi, N. *Empathy Dynamics: A Neuroscientific Perspective.* (2024).

Chapter 7

Korea's Role in UN PKO:
Fostering Peace in Moroccan Sahara

Ho Jae Shin (Kongju National University)

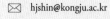 hjshin@kongju.ac.kr

Dr. Ho Jae Shin is a professor in the Department of Ethics Education at Kongju National University, where he teaches moral education, character education, and civic education. His academic interests lie in moral and political philosophy, as well as moral psychology, and he conducts research aimed at supporting the educational field. His key publications include *"A Study on the Framework Guiding the Direction of the National Character Education Policy"*, *"Exploring the Development and Issues of Representative and Participatory Democracy"*, and *"From Democratic Citizenship Education to Global Citizenship Education"*.

I. Introduction

Moroccan Sahara dispute remains one of the world's most enduring conflict zones, but quite different than other conflict zones that are characterized by armed struggles, since it is witnessing growing development in parallel of United Nations' effort to find a lasting political solution to the regional dispute.

The Republic of Korea has made substantial contributions to global peace and stability, initially providing military medical support to Morocco and later participating in UN Peacekeeping Operations (PKO). These efforts reflect Korea's growing global role and commitment as a UN member state. This paper examines Korea's PKO activities in Moroccan Sahara, highlighting their implications for international peace, sustainable cooperation, and Korea-Morocco relations.

II. Theoretical Foundations

1. History of the Moroccan Sahara Conflict

Moroccan Sahara, located on Africa's northwestern coast, borders, Algeria, and Mauritania. The region, historically under Spanish rule, gained geopolitical significance due to its abundant phosphate deposits.

Historically, the disputed region was neither *terra nullius* before Spanish rule in 1884, nor a separate entity from Morocco prior to colonization. In its 1975 ruling, the International Court of Justice (ICJ), affirmed that the Sahara's tribes had historical allegiance to Morocco's rulers. Then, the Sahara was recovered by Morocco in 1975, following the Madrid agreements which definitively put an end to the Spanish colonization of the region.

From 1884 to 1976, Spain controlled Moroccan Sahara, but its weakening political influence led to rising tensions. Morocco, Mauritania, and Algeria each laid claims to the region. Morocco, particularly proactive in asserting its position, labeled Spain a colonialist power and, in 1963, raised the issue at the UN. As Spain faced internal political instability in the early 1970s, Morocco intensified pressure, culminating in the 1975 Green March, where 350,000 Moroccan civilians mobilized into the region to assert sovereignty. Spain, rather than holding a UN-supervised referendum, reached an agreement to cede administrative control to Morocco and Mauritania.

Following Spain's withdrawal, the Polisario waged military campaigns against Moroccan and Mauritanian forces. By 1979, Mauritania had withdrawn, renouncing its claim, while Morocco retained its territory. The conflict persisted leading to an enduring territorial dispute (Chang, 2023).

The conflict remains unresolved, and the UN has been involved in peace negotiations, attempting to mediate between the parties and facilitate a fair and political settlement of the dispute.

2. The Conflict Impact and Intervention

The root cause of the Moroccan Sahara conflict lies in the dispute between Morocco and mainly the POLISARIO. However, due to the humanitarian impact, the UN became involved. While Article 2, Paragraph 7 of the UN Charter prohibits intervention in domestic matters, the UN engaged in the Moroccan Sahara conflict under the doctrine of the Responsibility to Protect (R2P) and the Security Council is actively addressing the matter under Chapter 6 of the Charter of the United Nations. This transformed the issue from a domestic into a regional dispute

Since the end of the Cold War, conflicts related to ethnicity, religion, territorial claims, and natural resources have increased worldwide, leading to a rapid expansion of UN peacekeeping operations (PKO). Before the 1990s, during the Cold War period, the UN conducted only about ten peacekeeping missions. However, between 1989 and 1994, over 20 new PKO missions were launched. Initially, UN peacekeeping focused on monitoring ceasefires, overseeing troop withdrawals, and patrolling buffer zones. Over time, their scope expanded to include election support, humanitarian assistance, and mine clearance.

In the context of Moroccan Sahara, UN efforts have reinforced ceasefire monitoring, election assistance, and humanitarian aid in the region. However, UN peacekeeping continues to face challenges due to the conflicting national interests of member States. The inherent tension between state sovereignty and collective security remains a persistent issue in international relations. Given this reality, UN peacekeeping efforts serve not as a definitive solution but as a means of fostering conditions conducive to resolution. Korea's PKO activities align with this perspective—not as direct conflict resolution efforts but as essential contributions to peacebuilding and diplomatic relations with Morocco.

3. Korea's Contributions to Stability in Moroccan Sahara

Korea's involvement in Moroccan Sahara is multifaceted, highlighting its role as a proactive global actor. By leveraging its enhanced international status and robust security capabilities, Korea has fostered cooperation with Morocco and contributed to regional stability. Since 1994, South Korea has deployed 42 medical support personnel annually to MINURSO. While this deployment ended in 2006, Korea continues to assist MINURSO as an observer (Lim, 2020).

Under the UN framework, Korea's participation in PKO in Moroccan Sahara underscores its commitment to maintaining international peace. The deployment of Korean personnel under the "UN Mission for the Referendum in Western Sahara" (MINURSO) exemplifies this dedication. MINURSO, established to oversee a peaceful referendum in the region, has played a pivotal role in transitioning the Moroccan Sahara conflict from a domestic issue to an international concern. Korea's support for MINURSO reflects its broader vision of sustainable peacekeeping (Shin, 2016).

A defining feature of Korea's PKO activities in Moroccan Sahara is their emphasis on sustainability. Effective international dialogue and cooperation thrive within multilateral frameworks, and the UN provides the optimal platform for such initiatives. Acting as a sovereign state rather than a UN member could risk infringing on national sovereignty and provoking political disputes. Korea's adherence to UN mandates ensures that its peacekeeping efforts remain neutral, sustainable, and widely supported by the international community.

4. Korea's PKO with UN Principles of Peacekeeping

Korea's PKO activities in Moroccan Sahara exemplify the UN's Principles of Peacekeeping, which emphasize the following (UN Peacekeeping):

Consent of the Parties: Korea maintains close communication with Morocco and other stakeholders to ensure the consent of all parties involved in peacekeeping efforts. UN peacekeeping operations are deployed only with the approval of the primary parties involved in the conflict, requiring their commitment to a political process. This consent ensures that the UN has both the political and operational freedom necessary to fulfill its mandate. Without such approval, peacekeeping missions risk becoming entangled in the conflict itself, potentially shifting toward enforcement actions rather than their core objective of maintaining peace. However, the consent of key parties does not automatically guarantee agreement at the local level, particularly if these parties are internally fragmented or lack effective control over their forces. Achieving broad-based consent becomes even more challenging in unstable environments where armed groups operate independently or where spoilers seek to disrupt the peace process.

Impartiality: Korea's role as a neutral mediator reinforces its commitment to fairness, enabling effective conflict resolution and fostering trust among involved parties. Impartiality is essential for securing the consent and cooperation of the main parties but should not be mistaken for neutrality or inaction. UN peacekeepers must remain impartial in their interactions with conflicting parties while actively enforcing their mandate. Similar to a fair referee who enforces rules without bias, a peacekeeping mission must not tolerate violations of the peace process or breaches of international norms and principles.

Upholding these standards is fundamental to its role. While maintaining positive relations with the parties is important, a peacekeeping operation must avoid any actions that could compromise its perceived impartiality. It should not hesitate to apply this principle rigorously, even in the face of potential misinterpretation or retaliation. Failing to uphold impartiality can weaken the mission's credibility and legitimacy, potentially leading to the withdrawal of consent from one or more parties, ultimately jeopardizing the operation's effectiveness.

Non-use of Force: Korea adheres to the principle of using force strictly for self-defense or to protect the mandate, operating within the UN framework to avoid escalating tensions. UN peacekeeping operations are not designed as enforcement mechanisms. However, with Security Council authorization, they may use force at the tactical level for self-defense and to uphold their mandate. In particularly unstable situations, the Security Council has granted peacekeeping missions "robust" mandates, allowing them to "use all necessary means" to prevent violent disruptions to the political process, protect civilians facing imminent threats, and support national authorities in maintaining law and order. Despite similarities in practice, robust peacekeeping should not be mistaken for peace enforcement as defined under Chapter VII of the UN Charter.

Robust peacekeeping involves the use of force at the tactical level with the authorization of the Security Council and consent of the host nation and/or the main parties to the conflict.

By contrast, peace enforcement does not require the consent of the main parties and may involve the use of military force at the strategic or international level, which is normally prohibited for Member States under Article 2(4) of the Charter, unless authorized by the Security Council.

A UN peacekeeping operation should resort to the use of force only as a last option. When force is necessary, it must be applied carefully, proportionally, and appropriately, adhering to the principle of using the minimum force required to achieve the desired outcome, while preserving the mission's consent and mandate. The use of force carries political consequences and may lead to unforeseen developments. Decisions about its use should be made at the appropriate level within the mission, taking into an account factors such as the mission's capabilities, public perception, humanitarian impact, protection of forces, the safety and security of personnel, and, most critically, how such actions may affect both national and local support for the mission.

Additionally, Korea has actively participated in PKO training programs and contributed expertise in post-conflict recovery, including rebuilding essential infrastructure and supporting civilian reintegration efforts. By upholding these principles, Korea ensures that its peacekeeping efforts align with international standards, contributing to the legitimacy and effectiveness of its mission in Moroccan Sahara.

5. Historical Foundations of Korea-Morocco Relations

Korea's commitment to peace is deeply rooted in its historical experiences. During the Korean War, international support, including the selfless service of Moroccan soldiers under the UN French Battalion, was instrumental in Korea's survival. This historical connection underscores the shared values of peace between Korea and Morocco.

The diplomatic relationship between the two nations, established in 1962, has flourished over the past six decades. Shared historical experiences, such as Korea's March First Independence Movement and Morocco's Green March, highlight their mutual pursuit of peace and independence. These parallels provide a robust foundation for continued collaboration in promoting peace and stability.

The March First Independence Movement of 1919 was a milestone in Korean history when the Korean people declared their country independent and raised awareness of humanitarian ideals, based on a code of conduct emphasizing peace and non-violence. The Constitution of the Republic of Korea stipulates that Koreans are "proud of their resplendent history and traditions dating from time immemorial, upholding the cause of the Provisional Republic of Korea Government born of the March First Independence Movement of 1919 and the democratic ideals of the April Nineteenth Uprising of 1960 against injustice." Specifically mentioned by the Constitution is the movement's role in helping lay the republic's foundation. To pay tribute to the spirit of the event as well as commemorate the movement's centennial anniversary, Koreans should continue working toward peace and reunification in accordance with the Proclamation of Korean Independence (Kocis, 2019).

Morocco's Green March was a symbolic and assertive move by Morocco to assert its historical claim to the Moroccan Sahara region as part of its pre-colonial territory. It effectively led to Spain's agreement to transfer administrative control of the Moroccan Sahara region, thereby marking a defining moment in restoring the territorial integrity of Morocco.

As Moroccans celebrate this significant event annually, they pay tribute to their country's enduring spirit and unity, reflecting on the past while considering the challenges and opportunities that lie ahead. A symbol of Morocco's historical legacy and its commitment to a just and lasting solution for the Moroccan Sahara region, the Green March remains a cornerstone of national pride and a topic of international significance. the Green March was a testament to Morocco's post-colonial pursuit of self-determination. This historic event, which transpired on November 6, 1975, is commemorated annually as a national holiday in Morocco on the same date (Morocco World News, 2023).

6. The Path Forward: Strengthening Korea-Morocco Collaboration

The enduring partnership between Korea and Morocco reflects their shared values and historical ties. Morocco's participation in the Korean War under the UN flag and Korea's contributions to peace and stability in Moroccan Sahara exemplify their mutual commitment to international cooperation. As Korea continues its peacekeeping efforts, it further strengthens the bond between the two nations and enhances their collaboration in addressing global challenges.

Future initiatives could include joint training programs, exchange of best practices in peacekeeping, and collaboration in humanitarian projects. Such endeavors would not only enhance the effectiveness of peacekeeping operations but also deepen bilateral relations between Korea and Morocco.

III. Conclusion

Korea's active participation in UN peacekeeping operations in Moroccan Sahara highlights its commitment to global peace and security. By supporting MINURSO, adhering to the Responsibility to Protect principle, and fostering sustainable cooperation within the UN framework, Korea demonstrates its dedication to conflict resolution and humanitarian values.

The historical connection between Korea and Morocco serves as a powerful reminder of their shared commitment to peace. As Korea continues its PKO activities, it not only contributes to the stability of Moroccan Sahara but also strengthens its ties with Morocco. These efforts underscore Korea's role as a responsible global actor, committed to promoting peace and stability in conflict zones worldwide. Through sustained collaboration, Korea and Morocco can further solidify their partnership and contribute to lasting peace in the region.

▪ References

Chang, S. W., A study on the Western Sahara conflict. Focusing on the conflict and current situation in Morocco and Polisario. *PKO Journal*, 27, 100-118. (2023).

Kocis, 2019. https://www.kocis.go.kr/eng/webzine/201902/sub05.html

Lim, S. C., After completing the Western Sahara observer mission (서부 사하라 옵서버 임무를 마치고). *PKO Journal*, 21, 165-176. (2020).

Morocco World News, 2023. https://www.moroccoworldnews.com/2023/11/358776/the-green-march-a-unique-chapter-in-post-colonial-moroccan-history

Shin, D. I., The conflict and current situation between Morocco and the Polisario Front over Western Sahara (서부 사하라를 둘러싼 모로코와 폴리사리오 간 분쟁 및 현황). *Institute of Foreign Affairs and National Security*, 2016, 1-4. (2016).

UN Peacekeeping. https://peacekeeping.un.org/en/principles-of-peacekeeping

United Nations. A new Partnership agenda. Charting a new horizon for UN

Peacekeeping. New York: United Nations. (2009).

United Nations. United Nations Peacekeeping Operations. Principles and Guidelines. New York: United Nations. (2008).

Chapter 8

Growing International Support for the Moroccan Sahara:
A path towards stability and development

Nouha Benjelloun Andaloussi (Korea University)

✉ nbenjelloun05@gmail.com

She is a PhD candidate at Korea University specializing in international cooperation, with a focus on colonial studies. Her research examines colonial heritage in Casablanca and the role of citizen participation. She holds dual Master's degrees in International Sciences and Comparative Analysis of Mediterranean Societies from the University of Turin (Italy) and Mohammed VI Polytechnic University (Morocco).

I. Introduction

On November 6, 2024, Morocco marked the forty-ninth anniversary of the Green March, a peaceful movement that led to the recovery of Western Sahara from Spain in 1975. In his annual address, King Mohammed VI reiterated the Moroccan identity of the Sahrawi population, their strong ties to the nation, and the country's ongoing dedication to enhancing their welfare. The increasing international recognition of Moroccan sovereignty over the Sahara, along with the growing support for Morocco's proposed Autonomy Initiative, extends beyond symbolic victories. As the King emphasized, the primary challenge now is to "continue promoting the development and progress of our southern provinces" (Morocco World News, 2024).

Morocco's approach is characterized by a combination of diplomatic engagement with global partners to secure recognition of its territorial integrity, while also focusing on the socio-economic development of the southern provinces. This dual strategy highlights the tangible benefits of economic integration for this disputed region. This paper argues that, from Morocco's perspective, international recognition of its territorial integrity represents a foundation for strengthening economic ties with both individual countries and regional organizations. Furthermore, Morocco's Autonomy Initiative reflects its commitment to integrating the southern provinces into both the national and global economies. To achieve this, international support is critical in accelerating access to African markets and fostering greater investment in the region.

II. Territorial integrity, stability and economic partnerships

Fixed borders are a strong incentive for the stabilization of the region. Waters (2015) makes three assumptions about territorial integrity, which deserves our attention with regards to the implications of recognizing the Moroccan Sahara as such.

First, territorial integrity promotes stability as it prevents violence and separatism which comes with the fracturing of territory. Second, it effectively helps reconcile differences among diverse communities. Rather than *othering* the population that falls in a gray area or outside the rule of the country, achieving territorial integrity is a starting point to manage and even promote cultural differences within the community at large. Thirdly, fixed borders reflect the value commitments of liberal international society better than any alternative. A strong and stable state has a higher capacity to engage in trade with partners in the international scene and attract economic investments.

The notion of democratic sovereignty is particularly relevant to the case studied in this paper. Weinert (2007) proposes a definition which reflects the changes in meanings of sovereignty throughout the years. He writes:

"Democratic Sovereignty "stabilizes" sovereignty as indicating in some significant sense supreme authority for and about a common good, and thus locates it within the ongoing, progressive struggle for democratic goods, human rights, and the extension of freedom." (Ibid, 112)

In fact, in the case of the Sahara, with the autonomy plan proposed by Morocco, the right to democracy and to security are granted to the Sahrawi population, which implies recognizing the legal supremacy of the Kingdom, while establishing freely elected institutions (IRES, 2023). In other words, the State would keep its prerogatives in foreign affairs and defense, in parallel with the creation of democratic institutions to manage regional economic, social, and cultural affairs. Additionally, southern provinces would benefit from funds for development where resources are insufficient.

This shifts our discussion to the potential of economic development in the southern provinces with the restoration of Morocco's territorial integrity, an element which partner countries must consider in the decision to recognize the Moroccan Sahara.

III. Implications of US, France, and Spain's recognition of the Moroccan Sahara

To date, 120 countries recognize the Moroccan Sahara, with more than 30 consulates present in Laayoune and Dakhla. When countries recognize each other's territorial integrity, this often involves agreements on trade, infrastructure, and resource management, all of which contribute to strengthening economic partnerships. For Morocco, where the monarchy—one of the oldest globally, alongside Japan's— and territorial integrity are non-negotiable principles, such recognition represents a milestone in its diplomatic efforts. The most significant recognitions of the Moroccan Sahara have come from the United States, France, and Spain. These developments have led to a deepening of ties with the United States and a reset in bilateral relations with France. In Spain's case, its historic recognition of the Moroccan Sahara serves as a symbolic conclusion to its period of occupation in the area prior to 1975.

1. The rapprochement with the United States

On December 10, 2020, US President Donald Trump issued the *Proclamation on Recognizing The Sovereignty Of The Kingdom Of Morocco Over The Western Sahara.* He declared that the United States "recognizes Moroccan sovereignty over the entire Western Sahara territory" and reaffirmed Morocco's autonomy plan as the only credible basis for resolving the conflict (White House, 2020). This recognition is a significant milestone for Morocco, given the U.S.'s role as the penholder of the UN Security Council resolution shaping negotiations over the Western Sahara. Additionally, this sets a strong precedent for U.S. allies, which is significant given the position of the United States in the international system order.

In 2021, during talks held in Washington between the U.S. Secretary of State Antony Blinken and Moroccan Foreign Minister Nasser Bourita, the U.S. reiterated its support. State Department spokesperson Ned Price emphasized shared goals of regional peace, security, and prosperity. Furthermore, the U.S. established a virtual diplomatic post in the Western Sahara, signaling plans to open a consulate, which would deepen bilateral ties.

This recognition aligns with the U.S.'s strategic interests in North Africa. Morocco's location along the Atlantic and Mediterranean and its proven capabilities positions it as a vital partner in defense and counterterrorism efforts (Ghoulidi, 2024). Additionally, the U.S. has economic incentives to invest in Morocco's Atlantic Initiative, which seeks to provide landlocked Sahel countries with access to the Atlantic Ocean. This initiative not only promotes regional economic integration but also aims to reduce conflicts in the region.

2. The reset in France-Morocco relations

France's recognition of the Moroccan Sahara marks another significant diplomatic milestone, signaling a reset after years of strained ties. Morocco's emphasis on territorial integrity was evident following its refusal of French aid after the 2023 earthquake (Zaaimi, 2023). Despite Morocco's post-independence close partnership with France, Morocco prioritized partnerships with countries supporting its sovereignty, such as Qatar, Spain, and the UAE, while also relying on its domestic capabilities. This approach underscored Morocco's diplomatic autonomy and its firm stance on partnerships aligned with its sovereignty.

This year, French President Emmanuel Macron addressed a letter to King Mohammed VI, affirming that "the present and future of Western Sahara fall within the framework of Moroccan sovereignty", and that France will act in accordance with this decision both at the national and international levels (Ministry of Foreign Affairs, African Cooperation and Moroccan Expatriates, 2024).

The letter was followed by President Macron's three-day state visit to Morocco, which culminated in his speech to the Moroccan parliament on October 29, carried significant political weight. This visit not only marked France's official recognition of the Moroccan Sahara, but also led to the signature of commercial and economic treaties and an official forum with entrepreneurs in Rabat.

The visit of the President, accompanied by a delegation of French ministers, entrepreneurs, and public figures, laid the groundwork for collaboration on key issues such as migration and visa policies, large-scale African development projects, and infrastructure initiatives. New cooperation areas have also emerged such as the video game industry and artificial intelligence.

3. Spain's recognition of the Moroccan Sahara: a symbolic move

As of 2024, Morocco ranks as Spain's third most important trade partner outside the EU, while Morocco is the 11th largest exporter to Spain (Atalayar, 2024). Spain's historical role as a former colonial power in Morocco and occupier of its Western Sahara until 1975, coupled with their geographical proximity, made it inevitable for Madrid to adopt a clearer stance on Morocco's territorial integrity. Indeed, as emphasized by Moroccan Head of Government Aziz Akhannouch, loyalty to Morocco's national cause—its territorial integrity—is a prerequisite for any country seeking to be a true ally (Hespress, 2022).

Following the U.S. recognition of the Moroccan Sahara, Morocco disclosed part of a 2022 letter from Spanish Prime Minister Pedro Sánchez. In the letter, Sánchez described Morocco's 2007 autonomy proposal for Western Sahara as "the most serious, realistic, and credible" framework for resolving the conflict. Sánchez also stressed in a press release the importance of transparency, avoiding unilateral actions, and maintaining constant communication in Spanish-Moroccan relations.

On April 7, 2022, King Mohammed VI and Sánchez released a joint declaration in Rabat reaffirming Spain's support, followed by a second declaration on February 2, 2023.

Spain's involvement in humanitarian aid, dialogue with Sahrawi population, and cooperation with UN agencies makes this shift in position particularly significant.

IV. Developments in regional organizations: the European Union, the Arab League and the African Union

1. Discrepancy between EU member states' positions and European Court of Justice rulings on trade agreements with Morocco

Within the European Union, many member states have expressed strong support for Morocco regarding the Western Sahara dispute, emphasizing Morocco's strategic importance as a key partner in Africa. In 2022, Germany recognized Morocco's autonomy proposal as a "good basis and a very good foundation" for resolving the conflict. This position was reinforced when German Foreign Minister Annalena Baerbock highlighted Morocco's "important role in the stability and sustainable development of the region." (Euractiv, 2022). Notably, Germany has also shown interest in Morocco's Royal Initiative, which aims to provide Sahel states with access to the Atlantic Ocean (Ministry of Foreign Affairs,

African Cooperation and Moroccan Expatriates, 2024).

Similarly, Denmark recognized the Moroccan Sahara and underscored Morocco's critical role in regional affairs, becoming the 18th European country to endorse Morocco's autonomy initiative. During a meeting on the sidelines of the UN General Assembly's high-level week on September 25, 2024, Moroccan Foreign Minister Nasser Bourita and Danish Foreign Minister Lars Løkke Rasmussen discussed Denmark's "Africa's Century" strategy and the Royal Initiative as part of their collaborative engagement with Africa (Ministry of Foreign Affairs, African Cooperation and Moroccan Expatriates, 2024).

2. Support for the Moroccan national cause within the Arab League and the African Union

Both the Arab League and the African Union, of which Morocco is a member, have made gestures reaffirming their support for Morocco's position on the Western Sahara, despite opposition from Algeria, a key backer of the Polisario.

In 2021, the Arab League, comprising 22 member states, officially adopted Morocco's unified map, which includes the southern provinces as part of Moroccan territory. This decision was explained as an acknowledgment of the need to respect Morocco's "geography" and "sovereignty" and to ensure the use of the accurate map in all official events (Panorient News, 2021). Additionally, the Gulf Cooperation Council

(GCC) has consistently expressed strong support for Morocco's territorial integrity, further reinforcing regional backing for Morocco's stance.

The African Union has recently demonstrated significant support for Morocco's position by excluding the Polisario from all meetings with international partners (Atalayar, 2024). This decision reflects the Union's stance of not recognizing it and its strong disapproval of the ongoing human rights violations in the Tindouf camps. This exclusion underscores the African Union's evolving approach to the Sahara issue.

These gestures from the Arab League and African Union signify a broader regional alignment with Morocco on the Western Sahara issue, underscoring its growing diplomatic influence within key Arab and African institutions.

V. The Republic of Korea (ROK)'s position on the Western Sahara: past and present

ROK-Morocco relations hold significant potential for growth, as highlighted by Moroccan Foreign Minister Nasser Bourita (The Korea Herald, 2024). Positioned strategically in East Asia and Africa, the two countries can serve as key bridges for enhancing intercontinental cooperation. Both nations are recognized on the international stage for their commitment to innovation—Korea for its rapid technological advancements and human capital development, and Morocco for its pioneering efforts in renewable energy and resource management.

In June 2024, Nasser Bourita and his Korean counterpart, Cho Tae-yul, met to explore opportunities for collaboration, particularly focusing on Morocco's Atlantic Coast Vision and its ambitious gas pipeline project, which aims to provide Sahel countries with greater access to energy resources. This meeting underscored the potential for Korea and Morocco to partner in advancing shared goals for sustainable development and regional connectivity.

To date, Korea maintains a neutral stance on the Sahara issue, adhering to international norms and U.N.-led efforts to resolve the conflict. However, stronger Korean involvement in the integration of Morocco's southern provinces into its economy is a possibility, given historical ties from the 1970s and ongoing exchanges of expertise. Notably, Daewoo Corporation played a pivotal role during the Green March, equipping participants with essential supplies such as tents, clothing, and footwear, despite challenging circumstances. This support came with the endorsement of President Park Chung-hee, who, on March 12, 1976, sent a letter to the late King Hassan II congratulating him on Morocco's victory and the return of its southern territories.

VI. The Autonomy Plan and the New Development Model for the Southern Provinces (NMDPS)

The autonomy plan proposed by Morocco in 2007 provides for the economic self-sufficiency of the Western Sahara. The government is also committed to allocating sufficient financial resources to the region for its development through investments in major sectors.

The Sahara territory could benefit from the current achievements in *the New Development Model for the Southern Provinces* launched in 2015 for southern provinces. Morocco invested hundreds of billions of US dollars in the region to establish them as a trade hub and connect them further with major production and distribution centers in the country and with African countries.

Among the milestones of the plan, we can mention the recent construction of the Sakia El Hamra Wadi Bridge, the establishment of new roads and airports in Laayoune and Dakhla, the Tiznit-Laayoune-Dakhla expressway project spanning 1055 kilometers, the desalination project against water scarcity, and the launch of the USD 20 billion Atlantic African Gas Pipeline Project, aimed at transporting gas from West Africa to Europe. Morocco has also addressed socio-economic and cultural challenges by investing in tourism and opening new healthcare institutions such as the new university hospital project in Laayoune.

VII. Conclusion: Morocco's potential as a trusted ally in Africa

Major powers, including the U.S, France and Germany among others, have aligned with Morocco by recognizing its sovereignty over the Western Sahara and the credibility of its proposed autonomy plan. This signaled growing trust in Morocco's strategic role in Africa and along the Atlantic. Discussions alongside the statements of recognition highlighted Morocco's potential to address critical challenges on the continent, such as security, water sufficiency, climate resilience, and green development.

Resolving the territorial dispute could not only reduce regional tensions but also grant Morocco greater freedom to enhance connectivity across Africa and improve its attractivity for foreign investments. Furthermore, Morocco's regional development initiatives in the southern provinces are expected to serve as pilot programs, offering valuable lessons for neighboring African countries.

■ References

AU–EU (2009), Etude de préfaisabilité de l'initiative Grande Muraille Verte pour le Sahara et le Sahel + Annexes. African Union–European Union.

Atalayar. "Spain and Morocco strengthen their trade ties", June 16, 2024. Accessed November 28, 2024. https://shorturl.at/wU1P1

Atalayar. "Heavy blow for Algeria: the African Union excludes the Polisario Front", July 24, 2024. Accessed November 28, 2024. https://shorturl.at/lIGXR

Al Jazeera. "EU–Morocco trade deals in Western Sahara ruled invalid, Rabat claims 'bias'", October 4, 2024. Accessed November 27, 2024. https://shorturl.at/IQGnR

Euractiv. "Morocco, Germany renew ties after 'misunderstandings', February 16, 2022.

Accessed November 28, 2024. https://shorturl.at/mdaik

Hespress. "Maroc-Espagne: Madrid ne semble pas vouloir franchir le pas vers la réconciliation", Janvier 21, 2022. Accessed November 28, 2024. https://fr.hespress.com/244473-244473.html

Morocco World News. "Green March: King Mohammed VI's Full Speech Addresses Outdated Narratives on Sahara." Morocco World News, November 6, 2024. Accessed November 20, 2024. https://www.moroccoworldnews.com.

Panorient News. "Arab League adopted unified map of Morocco", December 30, 2021. Accessed November 28, 2024. https://www.panorientnews.com/en/news.php?k=3019

The Korea Herald. "[Bridge to Africa] Morocco urges Korea to enhance cooperation in Atlantic coast vision", June 4, 2024. Accessed November 28, 2024. https://www.koreaherald.com/view.php?ud=20240604050576

Waters, T. W. (2015). "Taking the measure of nations: testing the global norm of territorial integrity", *Wisconsin International Law Journal*, Vol.33, No.3

Weinert, M. S. (2007). *Democratic Sovereignty Authority, legitimacy, and state in a globalizing age*, UCL Press

Ghoulidi, A. (2024). "Resetting U.S. West Africa Policy", April 29, 2024. Accessed November 22, 2024. https://www.heritage.org/africa/commentary/resetting-us-west-africa-policy

France Diplomacy. "Judgments by the Court of Justice of the EU on Western Sahara (04.10.24)". Accessed November 29, 2024. https://shorturl.at/5PywK

L'Institut Royale des Études Stratégiques (2023). *The White Book on Moroccan Sahara*

Ministry of Foreign Affairs, African Cooperation and Moroccan Expatriates (2024). "Statement by the Royal Office", July 30, 2024. Accessed November 20, 2024. https://diplomatie.ma/en/statement-royal-office-20

Ministry of Foreign Affairs, African Cooperation and Moroccan Expatriates (2024). "Morocco -Germany: Key points of the Joint Declaration", June 28, 2024.

Accessed November 20, 2024. https://diplomatie.ma/en/morocco-germany-key-points-joint-declaration

Ministry of Foreign Affairs, African Cooperation and Moroccan Expatriates (2024). "Morocco-Denmark: Joint Communiqué", July 30, 2024. Accessed November 20, 2024. https://diplomatie.ma/en/morocco-denmark-joint-communiqu%C3%A9

White House (2020). "Proclamation on Recognizing The Sovereignty Of The Kingdom Of Morocco Over The Western Sahara", December 10, 2020. Accessed November 21, 2024. https://trumpwhitehouse.archives.gov/

Zaaimi, S. "The Politics Behind Morocco Turning Down Help After the Devastating Earthquake." *Atlantic Council*. September 12, 2023. Accessed November 21, 2024. https://www.atlanticcouncil.org.

Chapter 9

A Vision for Multi-dimensional Mutual Growth Between Morocco and Korea

Tim Cheongho Lee (Sangmyung University)

✉ humantad@hanmail.net

Dr. Tim Cheongho Lee graduated from Seoul National University with a B.A., M.A., and Ph.D. in Ethics Education. He continued his education in the United States, where he received a Ph.D. in Philosophy from Southern Illinois University (Carbondale) in 2018. Dr. Lee is currently employed at Sangmyung University in Seoul, Korea, where he pursues his research interests in American Pragmatism and AI Ethics. His academic trajectory demonstrates a commitment to contributing to the growing dialogue in the fields of American pragmatism and AI ethics.

I. Introduction

Morocco and Korea have different historical, cultural, and economic origins, but their complementing capabilities allow them to work together rather successfully. Morocco is regarded as a promising nation with abundant natural resources and stable economic potential on the African continent. Morocco's strategic location at the meeting point of Africa, Europe, and the Middle East has shaped its economic and cultural development. With a rich history of migration, trade, and colonial influences, the country has developed a strong and varied economy. Morocco currently drives economic growth and international cooperation with its abundance of natural resources, industrial prowess, and cultural heritage. Its primary industries continue to grow with the support of both private investment and state-led initiatives, positioning the country as a major player in both domestic and international markets. To understand Morocco's economic and cultural landscape, one must examine the foundations of its development, the challenges it faces, and the strategies shaping its future. The goal of this study is to suggest some strategic ways that Korea and Morocco could cooperate to improve their cooperation.

II. Current State of Morocco

Morocco has a lengthy and ancient history, as evidenced by the thousands of years of Amazigh presence that has been documented there. In antiquity, the region was a crossroads of civilizations, and the Phoenicians, Carthaginians, and Romans all influenced the local culture. One significant turning moment was the arrival of Islam in the seventh century. Following the Islamic conquest, a number of powerful dynasties, most notably the Idrisids, Almoravids, Almohads, and Marinids, rose and fell, influencing Morocco's political and cultural character. A significant legacy of academia, art, and architecture was left by these dynasties (Bilgili & Weyel, 2009).

By solidifying authority within Morocco and extending their influence throughout North Africa and the Iberian Peninsula, these dynasties established connections and exchanges that continue to be significant today. Morocco's complex history has resulted in a unique cultural tapestry that blends native Berber, Andalusian, and Arab traditions.

Morocco's 1956 breakup with France was a watershed and the start of a new era. However, the newly independent nation has numerous challenges. These included developing a contemporary economy, managing complex international relations, promoting national cohesion, and setting up reliable political institutions. Among the challenges posed by colonial control were addressing social inequalities and integrating various populations.

1. Change and Political Stability

In Morocco, which is a constitutional monarchy, the king has considerable executive authority. As the nation struggled to define its post-colonial identity and power structures, the early years after independence were characterized by some political instability. But Morocco has become more politically stable over time, especially when compared to some of its neighbors in the area. The demand for more democratization and power sharing has intensified in recent decades notwithstanding these advancements. This has prompted continuous revisions meant to strike a balance between the monarchy's authority and the goals of a more democratic system of governance. These reforms have included steps to encourage greater accountability and openness in governance, as well as constitutional amendments and efforts to fortify civil society. The fact that these reforms are still under progress indicates that Morocco's political climate will continue to change.

2. Diversity and Social Change

Moroccan culture offers an intriguing fusion of modernity and heritage. Disparities still exist even though important progress has been made in increasing access to basic social services like healthcare and education. Particularly between urban and rural populations, social inequality is still a problem, and some groups are still marginalized. Access to resources, economic inequities, and historical circumstances are frequently the primary causes of these discrepancies. Comprehensive approaches emphasizing social inclusion, economic development, and education are needed to address these problems.

Another diverse country is Morocco, which is home to a wide range of civilizations, ethnic groups, and religious traditions. The diverse cultural mosaic is influenced by Arabs, Berbers, and other ethnic groups. Although other religions are also practiced, Islam is the most common. Although this diversity is a strength, it also necessitates careful consideration in order to promote openness, tolerance, and respect for one another. It takes communication, understanding, and a dedication to equal rights and opportunities for all citizens to create a unified national identity that celebrates this diversity.

3. International Cooperation and Foreign Relations

Morocco has a complicated web of foreign policy issues to deal with.

One of the key points of concern is the long-standing territorial dispute in its Sahara. Morocco's security and diplomatic endeavors are also impacted by regional crises and instability in its neighbors. Through diplomatic channels, the nation actively seeks peace and stability, working to strengthen ties with its neighbors and interacting with the international community on a variety of topics. Morocco's economic objectives are reflected in its foreign policy, which aims to forge alliances and draw in international capital. The nation actively participates in regional and global organizations, helping to tackle issues like economic development, climate change, and terrorism.

Morocco has made great strides since gaining its independence, but there are still many obstacles to overcome. In a number of important areas, persistent efforts are essential. To strengthen democracy, guarantee increased involvement, and encourage accountability, more political reforms are required. In order to solve unemployment and poverty, economic development must be sustainable and inclusive, generating opportunity for all facets of society. To close the gaps between various groups and guarantee that all residents have access to opportunities and necessary services, more social integration is necessary. Last but not least, negotiating the intricate global environment calls for deft diplomacy and a dedication to amicable dispute settlement. To ensure Morocco's long-term peace, prosperity, and ongoing advancement on the international scene, these complex issues must be resolved.

III. Morocco's Potential and Strengths

Because of their complementary capabilities, Morocco and Korea have a great deal of potential for cooperation despite their different historical, cultural, and economic backgrounds. With its advantageous location in northwest Africa, Morocco acts as a crucial link between Europe, Africa, and the Middle East, providing substantial benefits for investment, trade, and logistics. This strategic location, together with Morocco's wealth of natural resources, steady economic growth, comparatively stable political climate, and steady infrastructure development, solidifies Morocco's position as a major player in regional and international markets and attracts foreign investment. In the meantime, Korea's cutting-edge technology and vibrant cultural sectors have had a significant influence on the world market. By utilizing Korea's technological know-how and creativity in conjunction with Morocco's geographic and economic advantages, strategic collaboration between the two countries might promote mutual growth and result in long-term economic and diplomatic gains for both.

1. Plenty of Resources

Morocco's wealth of natural resources provides a solid foundation for its economy. Importantly, it has the greatest phosphate rock reserves in the world, which makes it a major provider of fertilizers based on phosphate. Phosphate exports are a major source of national income, making this resource a vital component of the Moroccan economy. For Morocco to continue to prosper economically, this resource must be developed and managed.

Morocco has a strong agricultural sector in addition to its mineral resources. Important commodities including wheat, grapes, and olives may be grown there thanks to its varied climate and abundant ground. Both local consumption and exports, especially to markets in Europe and the Middle East, are bolstered by these agricultural products. Nonetheless, the agricultural industry has difficulties, such as uneven barley and potato crop yields brought on by climate change and fluctuating weather patterns, as well as comparatively low cattle farming productivity. Sustainable agricultural policies and technology developments are required to address these problems in order to increase productivity, guarantee food security, and optimize the sector's economic contribution.

2. Development of Industry

Morocco has developed into a major industrial hub during the last 20 years, especially in the fields of manufacturing and renewable energy. Particularly noteworthy is the automobile sector, which is expanding quickly thanks to Morocco's affordable workforce and robust government assistance. Numerous automakers from Europe have set up production facilities, especially at Kenitra, which is close to Rabat. Tax reductions and infrastructure upgrades are examples of government incentives that draw in foreign investment. Morocco is positioned as a major player in the regional and international automotive markets thanks to its expanding automotive industry.

Morocco has advanced significantly in the field of renewable energy as well. Its expansive desert terrain and powerful coastal breezes make it the perfect place to capture wind and solar energy. Significant investments in massive solar farms, wind energy projects, and geothermal exploration are helping the government reach its objective of producing 40% of its electricity from renewable sources by 2030 (Ourya & Abderafi, 2023). One of the biggest solar power facilities in the world, the Noor Ouarzazate Solar Complex, is a prime example of Morocco's dedication to sustainable growth and renewable energy. In addition to meeting domestic energy needs, Morocco's emphasis on renewable energy establishes the country as a regional leader and creates prospects for technological cooperation and exports (Ourya & Abderafi, 2023). Morocco's industrial development is further supported by its policy of privatization in specific areas and its comparatively liberal economy, which is driven by supply and demand. This is further supported by the fact that it is a leading economy by GDP (PPP) and a significant role in African economic affairs.

3. Tourism and Culture

An important advantage of Morocco is its rich cultural legacy, a colorful tapestry influenced by Berber, Roman, Arab-Islamic, French, and Spanish elements. Its architecture, food, music, and customs all reflect this varied past, making it a crossroads of cultures that welcomes millions of visitors each year. With a significant impact on GDP and employment, tourism is an essential part of the Moroccan economy. From the Sahara Desert to the Atlas Mountains and Mediterranean coastlines, the nation's varied landscapes appeal to a broad spectrum of traveler interests. The vibrant markets of Marrakech, the historic medinas of Fez, and the picturesque seaside towns of Tangier and Essaouira are all popular tourist destinations. Morocco's allure is increased by UNESCO World Heritage Sites including the ancient city of Meknes and the Roman ruins of Volubilis.

One of the most significant economic areas in Morocco is tourism, which is centered on the nation's history, culture, and coastline. With 14.5 million foreign tourists and MAD 104.7 billion in revenue, 2023 set a new record for tourism, surpassing the average number of visitors in the 2010s. The goal of the government's Vision 2020 strategy is to rank Morocco among the top 20 travel destinations in the world. Morocco's culture, including its historic towns, is attracting more and more tourists, who take advantage of the country's landscape, cultural heritage, and ancient and Islamic attractions. A popular beach resort,

Agadir serves as a starting point for trips to the Atlas Mountains. There are more well-liked resorts in northern Morocco. Morocco is marketed as an affordable, unique, and secure travel destination through extensive government-sponsored advertising efforts. The majority of visitors are from Europe, and a sizable percentage are French. The main port for cruise ships is Casablanca. A well-liked destination in Marrakech is the Majorelle botanical park. The regions with the quickest growth include activity and adventure tourism in the Atlas and Rif Mountains. The government is making investments in desert tourism and trekking routes. In order to promote cultural interchange and tourism growth, Morocco has also fortified its international tourism relations, such as a 1993 visa-exemption agreement with Korea. As a result, more Korean tourists are traveling to Morocco, and interest in Korean culture there is also rising.

Beyond tourism, Morocco boasts a rich cultural legacy that includes architecture, literature, music, film, food, and sports. Its architecture combines elements of Islamic architecture, local vernacular styles, old Roman sites, and contemporary influences. Moroccan literature has a long history and was especially prominent during the Almoravid and Almohad empires. It is produced in a variety of languages. One important literary hub has been the University of al-Qarawiyyin in Fes. Moroccan music includes a wide range of styles due to its diverse origins. Additionally, the nation boasts a thriving film industry. Morocco's cosmopolitan past is reflected in its cuisine, which is regarded as one of the most varied in the world. Another significant aspect of Moroccan culture is sports, especially football.

IV. Korea's Advantages and Prospects for Collaboration

Korea and Morocco have maintained a friendship and cooperative relationship since the two countries established diplomatic ties in 1962, especially in the fields of industrial, technological, and cultural exchanges. With plenty of chances to strengthen bilateral ties and capitalize on each nation's advantages, this long-standing partnership offers a strong basis for future cooperation enhancement in a number of areas.

1. Collaboration between Industry and Technology

Morocco's economic development can benefit greatly from Korea's well-known industrial competitiveness and strong technological capabilities, especially in sectors like manufacturing, energy, and infrastructure.

In Morocco, Korea's proficiency in planning and constructing intricate infrastructure projects has already been advantageous. The 2022 contract given to Korea's National Railroad Corporation for the design of a portion of Morocco's high-speed rail system serves as a noteworthy illustration. The possibility for additional collaboration in infrastructure development is demonstrated by this initiative. Beyond rail, Korea can use its top-notch technologies to help improve other vital infrastructure, including roads, ports, airports, and urban infrastructure. The expansion of Morocco's infrastructure may be greatly aided by the transfer of technology and expertise in the areas of project management, construction techniques, and sustainable practices.

In Morocco, Korean goods are highly valued, especially electronics and cars. By developing local production bases, there is a great chance to expand on this popularity. Partnerships between Moroccan and Korean businesses could lead to the development of high-tech production facilities for electronics, cars, and other items. Technology transfer, cooperative R&D projects, and the exchange of manufacturing best practices are a few examples of this kind of cooperation. This would improve Morocco's industrial sector's long-term growth and competitiveness globally, in addition to generating job prospects (Kim & Lee, 2013).

Korea's cutting-edge renewable energy technologies in fields like solar and wind power offer Morocco substantial prospects for collaboration as it continues its energy transition. Together, the two nations may build more wind and solar power plants and increase Morocco's capability for renewable energy. In order to improve the dependability and effectiveness of Morocco's renewable energy systems, Korea can provide cutting-edge technologies including grid integration systems and energy storage solutions. Joint ventures in the production of green hydrogen, a developing field with enormous promise for both nations, may also be part of this partnership.

Korea's dominance in ICT technologies, such as cybersecurity, smart cities, and 5G networks, offers Morocco significant prospects for collaboration in its digital transformation. Korea can help Morocco strengthen cybersecurity frameworks, improve digital governance systems, and create smart cities. Furthermore, Morocco's innovation in technology-driven industries can be supported by utilizing Korea's proficiency in artificial intelligence and the Internet of Things (IoT). The creation of innovation and research hubs to aid in the expansion of Morocco's digital economy may be a component of this partnership.

2. Intercultural Communication

A solid foundation for expanding cultural exchange between Morocco and Korea is provided by the rising popularity of Korean pop culture in Morocco. Korea and Morocco can develop stronger social and cultural relations by fostering mutual understanding through cooperation and the sharing of cultural content.

The introduction of Korean pop culture, such as K-pop, K-drama, and Korean cinema, to Morocco and the exchange of Moroccan cultural content with Korea are two of the most promising paths for cultural interaction. Mutual respect could be strengthened by producing tailored cultural content that enhances Korean comprehension of Moroccan customs and art while appealing to Moroccan audiences' inclinations.

Cultural interaction can be further facilitated by projects like art exhibitions, music festivals, and co-producing movies and television series.

Organizing a range of cultural events, including exhibitions, performances, and festivals, can give both countries a firsthand look at one another's cultures. By providing venues for interaction and engagement between artists, performers, and spectators, events such as the Moroccan Arts Festival in Korea and the Korean Film Festival in Morocco can highlight the depth and diversity of both nations' cultural heritage. These kinds of gatherings have the potential to establish avenues for cultural diplomacy that strengthen ties between Morocco and Korea.

Creating internships, academic collaborations, and student exchange programs can all contribute to strengthening educational and cultural linkages. These programs promote an awareness of language, customs, and traditions by giving young people, academics, and artists the opportunity to see different countries firsthand. Additionally, academic partnerships between colleges in both nations can delve deeper into fields like social sciences, art history, and cultural studies, which would promote intercultural cooperation and learning.

The chance to co-host the FIFA World Cup in 2030 offers a special opportunity to advance cultural diplomacy in addition to sporting relations. Both nations can promote bilateral tourism and highlight their cultural treasures by working together to organize events. Through sporting events, cultural displays, and shared experiences, the World Cup may serve as a platform for promoting respect for one another.

3. Cooperation in Infrastructure Development

Morocco's rapid infrastructure development and urbanization present many potential for cooperation with Korea, whose knowledge in smart technologies and sustainable development might be extremely helpful to Morocco's expanding cities.

Morocco's urban growth can be modeled after Korea's achievements in creating smart cities, including the Songdo International Business District. Both nations may collaborate to build more habitable, sustainable, and efficient cities by integrating smart technologies into Morocco's urban infrastructure. Modern communication networks, energy-efficient structures, and sophisticated transit systems may all be included into these smart cities, improving the standard of living for citizens and lessening their negative effects on the environment.

Korea can take part in a range of infrastructure projects in Morocco by using PPP models, including healthcare, educational, and transportation networks (Kim & Lee, 2013). These methods would increase the participation of Korean businesses in Morocco's infrastructure development by enabling the public and private sectors to share risk and investment. Additionally, using Korea's experience in overseeing major projects can guarantee these endeavors are completed successfully and on schedule.

The adoption of new technologies in infrastructure development can be expedited by Korea and Morocco working together to create and accept technical standards. Project efficiency and effectiveness can be significantly increased, expenses can be decreased, and the highest quality requirements can be met by bringing both countries' technological norms into alignment. This cooperation can be extended to a number of industries, such as transportation, telecommunications, and construction, strengthening Korea and Morocco's technological alliance.

4. Improving Trade and Economic ties

Korea and Morocco must improve their economic collaboration, especially in areas like resource-technology integration, industrial diversification, and investment, in order to optimize the potential for mutual growth.

Both nations can foster industrial development and technical innovation by fusing Morocco's wealth of natural resources, including minerals and phosphates, with Korea's technological know-how. For instance, the processing and value-added production of Moroccan natural resources can be improved by Korea's cutting-edge manufacturing technology, which would help Morocco's economy diversify and create jobs (Seo & Seo, 2022).

Morocco can speed up its economic development by learning from Korea's experience diversifying its industries, which range from electronics to advanced manufacturing and biotechnology. Korea may aid Morocco with diversifying its economy and lowering its reliance on a small number of industries by supporting the country's development of new industries, especially in the areas of technology, high-value manufacturing, and renewable energy.

Increased investment flows can result from fortifying investment agreements and enhancing the economic climate in both nations. Korea and Morocco can both encourage sustainable economic growth by offering incentives and assistance for bilateral investments. In order to draw investment in important areas like infrastructure, renewable energy, and ICT, this involves fostering collaborations between governmental bodies, financial institutions, and private businesses.

V. In conclusion

Morocco and Korea have a lot of potential for cooperation and complementary strengths in a number of areas, including infrastructure, industry, technology, and culture. Both countries may promote mutual prosperity by utilizing Morocco's wealth of resources and industrial potential in conjunction with Korea's technological prowess and cultural vibrancy. In addition to promoting both nations' economic, technical, cultural, and infrastructure advancement, increasing cooperation in these fields will increase their influence internationally. Bilateral relations will be further strengthened by ongoing communication and strategic alliances that involve information sharing and cultural exchange, laying the groundwork for future prosperity and long-term progress.

■ References

Bilgili, Ö., & Weyel, S. (2009). Migration in Morocco: History, current trends and future prospects. *Paper Series: Migration and development country profiles*, 1-62.

Hwang, K. D. (2014). Korea's soft power as an alternative approach to Africa in development cooperation: Beyond economic interest-led perspectives of Korea-Africa relations?. *African and Asian Studies*, 13(3), 249-271.

Kausch, K. (2009). The European Union and political reform in Morocco. *Mediterranean politics*, 14(2), 165-179.

Kim, J. H., & Lee, J. S. (2013). Export-driven Industrial Development in Morocco: Prospects for Korean-Morocco Partnership: Prospects for Korean-Morocco Partnership. 한국아프리카학회지, 39, 133-159.

Ourya, I., & Abderafi, S. (2023). Clean technology selection of hydrogen production on an industrial scale in Morocco. *Results in engineering*, 17, 100815.

Park, D. Y. (2002). A Comparative Study on the Patterns of Economic Development and Trade in Korea and Morocco. *International Area Review*, 5(1), 81-110.

Rossi, A. (2011). Economic and social upgrading in global production networks: The case of the garment industry in Morocco (Doctoral dissertation, University of Sussex).

Seo, D., & Seo, B. (2022). Advancement plan into economic soft power for multifaceted trade in Morocco, North Africa. *The Journal of the Convergence on Culture Technology*, 8(5), 103-110.

Steenbruggen, John. 2016. Tourism geography: Emerging trends and initiatives to support tourism in Morocco. *Journal of Tourism & Hospitality,* 3, 224-39.

Willis, M., & Messari, N. (2003). Analyzing Moroccan foreign policy and relations with Europe. *The Review of International Affairs,* 3(2), 152-172.

Chapter 10

Strengthening Relationships between South Korea and Morocco:
Mutual Cooperation through the promotion of treatment
for Moroccan veterans of the Korean War

Hyunsoo KIM (Pusan National University)

✉ hans.kim@pusan.ac.kr

Dr. Hyunsoo Kim is an Associate Professor in the Department of Ethics Education & Director of Graduate Program of International Education Development Cooperation Major at Pusan National University (PNU), Pusan, Republic of Korea. In 2002 he got his Ph. D. from Seoul National University, Korea. He has taught Applied Ethics such as Biomedical Ethics and AI Ethics, together with Moral Education curriculum and teaching & learning since 2019. Before joining PNU, he was a research fellow at the Korea Institute of Curriculum and Evaluation. He is the author of several books, including Biomedical Ethics, Marriage and Family Ethics, Business Ethics in Current Society, Contractualism and Deontology (all in Korean), and others. His Current research interests are International Relations, Applied Ethics especially on AI Ethics, Moral Psychology, Moral Education. Now he is an Editor in chief of Korea Association for Public Value which has published Journal of Public Value since June 2021.

Wonseok Bang (Gyeongsang National University)

✉ bangws@daum.net

Dr. Bang holds a doctorate in Business Administration from Gyeongsang National University and is currently a Research Professor at the Center for Entrepreneurship Studies. He earned a Master's degree in Business Administration from Sogang University and graduated from the Korea Air Force Academy. He is a member of the Jinju K-Entrepreneurship Committee (Present), a member of the Korean Institute for Global Entrepreneurship Research (Present), and a vice president of the Korean Society for Safety Culture (Present). Major publications are as followings: *Entrepreneurship and Visionary Startups for Corporate Sustainability*, Pakyoungsa (2023), *Malvin Berkowitz's PRIMED Character Education Theory* (Co-author), Kyoyookgwahaksa (2024) etc.

I. Introduction

The Korean War began with the invasion of the South by the North Korean army on June 25, 1950, and lasted for 3 years, 1 month, and 2 days until the armistice was signed on July 27, 1953(National Archives of Korea, 2024). Many countries in the UN helped the Republic of Korea during the Korean War. The number of countries participating in the Korean War was 16 until early 1951. Of the 21 countries that applied to send troops, the 16 countries that sent troops were the following: the United States and Canada (2 in North America), Colombia (1 in South America), Australia, New Zealand, the Philippines, and Thailand (4 in Asia), South Africa and Ethiopia (2 in Africa), and the United Kingdom, Belgium, France, Greece, Luxembourg, the Netherlands, and Turkey (7 in Europe). As of 1953, the main participating troops were about 14,200 from the UK, about 6,100 from Canada, about 5,500 from Turkey, and about 2,200 from Australia. By 1953, the total number of Allied

Forces participating in the Korean War was about 39,000, excluding the US, and about 341,000 including the US. Further, member states and international organizations began to provide various types of support by the UN resolution, with five countries (Sweden, India, Denmark, Norway, and Italy) providing medical support such as hospitals or hospital ships, and 40 member states, one non-member state (Italy), and nine UN specialized agencies participating in food provision and civilian relief activities (National Archives of Korea, 2024).

However, the most recent, new fact discovered that some military soldiers from Morocco attended the Korean War. These facts have not been revealed because their nationality at that time was France. At the time, Morocco was a French protectorate and they participated in the war as part of the UN French Battalion (Sege newspaper, 2024).

Moreover, Morocco has maintained friendly relations with Korea since establishing diplomatic relations in July 1962. In September of that year, Korea was the first to open a resident embassy in Morocco on the African continent. Since that time, the two countries have developed a relationship in several areas such as social security, economic partnership. In 2022, Korea and Morocco celebrated the 60th anniversary of diplomatic relations between the two countries through various events (Seoul City Newspaper, 2024). Further, since July 2021, through the cooperation of Morocco and government agencies, Korea has been able to re-examine the forgotten history and meaning of the two countries by officially discovering the first Moroccan Korean War veteran. Korean government has made all efforts to support foreign military soldiers who attended the Korean War. In the view of the same, the Korean government needs to serve the Moroccan Korean War veteran who was newly discovered.

Therefore, this paper aims to provide several practical suggestions for how the Korean government serves the Morocco foreign military veterans of the Korean War.

II. Relationship between South Korea and Morocco

1. Moroccan Soldiers' Participation in the Korean War

During the Korean War of 1950, soldiers from Morocco participated in the war. At the time, Morocco was a French protectorate and they participated in the war as part of the UN French Battalion. It has been officially confirmed that many soldiers from Morocco in North Africa fought in the Korean War. Following the first two confirmed to be buried at the United Nations Memorial Cemetery in Korea(UNMCK) last year (see Fig. 1), the identities of additional veterans are being confirmed one after another(Busan newspaper, 2022).

Moreover, The Korean Embassy in Morocco announced on November 15, 2022, that it had additionally confirmed the identities of six Moroccan Korean War veterans. Earlier, late last year, it had checked the UNMCK's data and found Gian Julien, a Jewish, and Mohamed

Lasri, a Muslim, among the unknown soldiers who died in 1953. The information on the six people confirmed this time has not yet been made public. The embassy said, "We have also secured a list of 16 additional possible participants and are currently confirming them." Morocco was a French protectorate during the Korean War and participated in the war wearing French military uniforms. As a result, the work to confirm the veterans was difficult, but it gained momentum last year when Ambassador keeyong-chung heard from the French Embassy in Morocco that the data remained in the French Military Archives (Busan newspaper, 2022).

Fig. 1. Tombstone of a Moroccan war veteran buried at the Busan UNMCK.

Meanwhile, UNMCK has a service that allows you to find the records of the fallen soldiers. If you find these records, you can find the records of the last days of the fallen soldiers. According to the records, Julien Djian died on July 4, 1953, and Mohamed Landri died on July 18, 1952. The records of the two soldiers stored at UNMCK are as shown in Fig. 2. Together with this, In addition, the UNMCK website offers Hero of the Day, Tributary Message, and Online Flower Dedication services to help you remember and commemorate veterans.

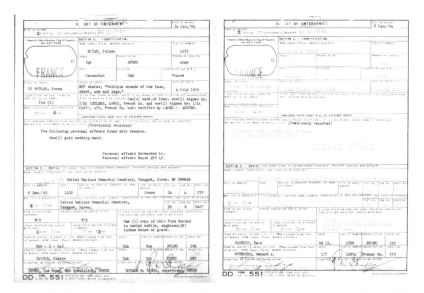

Fig. 2. Official document of Burial Report of Moroccan veterans who attended in Korean War.

Separately, recent research has additionally provided the names of six Moroccan soldiers who died in the Korean War: Belkacem BELHAROURI, Omar LASSOUED, Brahim ZAMORI, Youssef ELBARBI ABDI, Ali BELMOKHTAR, and Mohamed HAMROUNI (Ambassade de la Republique de Coree a Rabat, 2022). Since they are not buried at UNMCK, their deeds need to be shed light on them based on more detailed original records.

2. Extensive relationship between South Korea and Morocco

Established diplomatic relations between South Korea and Morocco in 1962, there are some main events for both countries' relationship in history below. In fact, after 2000, both countries generally have an extensive relationship in terms of economic, social, medical, etc. Practically, the relationship between Korea and Morocco began to grow in the 2000s, and the number of Korean tourists visiting Morocco is increasing. Korea and Morocco have a visa- free policy.

International education development cooperation between Korea and Morocco is actively being carried out through the partner cooperation projects of the Korea International Cooperation Agency (KOICA). Representative examples include energy efficiency projects, youth mid-term volunteer group dispatch projects, Rabat public transportation-centered eco-friendly transportation system construction projects, and maternal and child health projects for health equity in the Beni Mellal region. In addition to these representative examples, various forms of exchange are expanding.

III. Suggestions for Strengthening Relationships between South Korea and Morocco Mutual Cooperation

1. Efforts on the Social Aspects

According to Article 4-2 of the Republic of Korea Act (UN Forces Participation Day), the country commemorates the sacrifices and achievements of the UN participating countries and veterans. It passes them on to future generations by designating July 27, the anniversary of the Korean War Armistice Agreement, as UN Forces Participation Day (United Nations Veterans Act, 2023). Based on the United Nations Veterans Act, the Korean government invites veterans and their families to repay their scarifications and support some diverse programs such as taking a tour of Panmunjom and the 38th Parallel tour.

In this context, this paper proposes several suggestions for honoring Morocco veterans and promoting a friendly relationship with Morocco. First, according to the basic objectives and direction of promotion of policies for honoring UN veterans, Korea should make all efforts to support their sacrifice. Therefore, it is necessary to invite the families of Moroccan veterans to commemorative events and memorial services for veterans and to allow them to be buried in the UN cemetery along with other UN veterans if they so desire.

Second, Moroccan veterans and their families must be invited to participate in programs that allow them to experience the 38th parallel, the site of Korea's division, the War Memorial, and Korea's economic development. This kind of program could be enhanced their psychological self-respect to veterans themselves and their children, so they are very pleased to see Korea's development like their country due to participating to keep the freedom from enemies. It is the small reward to their scarification, and then this kind of program need to be expended more.

Third, to honor the noble sacrifices of Moroccan veterans and contribute to the promotion of friendly cooperation with the participating countries at the national level, we must run a scholarship program to provide the descendants of veterans from UN participating countries including Morocco with the opportunity to study in Korea and to support them to grow as close people based on this. Further, if descendants of veterans want to join the Korean military, the Korean government prepares for the institutional policy doing so.

Lastly, identifying the Moroccan veterans is also good news for verifying the participation of other small countries, which is only speculated. As it becomes known that identification is not impossible, each country can provide information and report on the bereaved families. According to the UNMCK, 104 of the 2,319 veterans currently buried in the park are 'unknown soldiers' whose identities have not been confirmed. The nationality of four of them has not been confirmed. There may be cases like Morocco where they joined the military of another country to participate in the war. According to basic objectives and direction of promotion of policies for honoring UN veterans, Korea should sustainably exhume veterans' remains and conducting DNA tests are also included.

1. Efforts on the Educational Aspects

In order to further strengthen mutual cooperation between Korea and Morocco, it would be effective to approach it in the direction of implementing international understanding education for the next generation of youth. In particular, educating the next generation about the contributions of Moroccan veterans to Korea's development will be an important factor in the continued growth of social development and exchange experiences between the two countries. Such educational efforts can be concretized by exploring ways to reflect them in the public education system, especially in elementary and secondary schools. This is because practical educational effects can be expected through educational activities carried out in the context of school education.

There are many things to introduce about Morocco's contributions to Korea. And the categories can be set in various areas such as politics, diplomacy, economy, society, and culture. However, the most effective and practical way to teach Morocco's contributions is to utilize the special structure of moral education. This method can be found in the following three ways.

1.1. Cross-Curricular Learning Topics

It is to educate Morocco's contribution to Korea through teaching and learning of cross-curricular learning topics in the national curriculum. Cross-curricular learning topics are learning contents that are required by the country and society, and are comprehensive and integrated learning topics that cross the boundaries of various subjects. The 2022 revised curriculum currently in use sets 10 cross-curricular learning topics. Cross-curricular learning topics are to be dealt with in an integrated manner across all educational activities, including subjects and creative experiential activities, and are recommended to be taught in conjunction with local communities and families. However, in order to more effectively educate Morocco's contribution to Korea through these cross-curricular learning topics, it is necessary to extract achievement standards and content elements related to them, develop and present examples of learning models and teaching and learning materials related to them, and distribute them so that they can be used more conveniently in schools.

A specific example of a method of teaching Morocco's contribution to Korea through teaching and learning of cross-curricular learning topics can be a method that utilizes the moral storytelling class model. Examples of the Teaching and Learning model and materials according to the stages of the moral storytelling class model can be presented as follows.

Step	Contents
Learning problem recognition and motivation	Learn about cooperation and the development of our country through the sacrifices of our friends' countries.
Presentation of moral stories and understanding of main contents	Stories about the sacrifice of Moroccan veterans
Exploration of moral stories and presentation and sharing of one's own moral experiences	Students shares opinions of what they feel about the sacrifice and service of Moroccan warriors.
Composition of one's own moral stories or similar imaginary stories	Students create a similar hypothetical moral tale from the perspective of a Moroccan veteran.
Organization and expansion of application and practical application in daily life	Explore ways to convey lessons and gratitude in everyday life.

Table 1. Steps of Moral Storytelling of the sacrifice of Moroccan veterans

1.2. Occasional Education: Education that takes place during special times

Occasional education is education on a specific topic that is not presented in the school curriculum. It is conducted in the form of covering a specific anniversary or a topic with current meaning. In particular, Korea commemorates Memorial Day on June 6 and the Korean War that broke out on June 25. Therefore, through the development and use of occasion education materials for June, which is the month of patriotism and veterans, it is possible to educate about Morocco's contributions to Korea.

1.3. Use as special material for textbook development

Korean textbooks are produced by publishers and are subject to government inspection. Therefore, they reflect the achievement standards of the curriculum, but some autonomy of the developers is guaranteed.

Therefore, it is effective for publishers and textbook authors to provide excavated materials and actively promote them so that the contributions of Moroccan warriors can be reflected in textbooks in the form of anecdotes or learning materials. In particular, methods such as reflecting them in the form of anecdotes in the main text of the textbook, presenting them in the form of learning materials in the margins on both sides, or reflecting them in the activity section at the end can be explored. Examples of such materials can be seen in Fig. 3.

Fig. 3. Middle school <Ethics> textbook material containing Global Citizenship & Ethics

In particular, the provision of these materials requires the creation and distribution of detailed and practical lesson plans, videos, and other learning materials that can be used immediately in school classrooms.

This is because only by doing so can we reduce the burden on teachers in the field and increase their usability in school settings.

IV. Conclusion

Korea has made all effort to strengthen to support for UN veterans. Beyond the limited support for veterans, Korea need to approach diplomatic and economic relationships of participating countries including Morocco. Namely, Korea has made their commitment to enhancing bilateral ties and exploring new avenues for cooperation.

Most recent, overall, Korea and Morocco signed three agreements in June 2024, with one focusing on social security to address specific challenges faced by Korean and Moroccan nationals, providing protection based on equality, reciprocity, and the preservation of rights. In conclusion, the determination of Korea and Morocco to bolster bilateral ties is evident in their recent engagements and agreements. By focusing on key areas such as trade, investment, social security, and climate change, both nations are paving the way for a more prosperous and collaborative future. This renewed partnership is not only beneficial for Korea and Morocco but also holds promise for broader regional and global cooperation.

This is a policy to reward the sacrifices and contributions of UN veterans including Morocco in the Korean War and to continue and develop friendly relations with the Morocco as well as other UN participating countries. Therefore, our future of relative countries pursues the higher value such as freedom and quality of their life beyond the thanks for their scarifications.

■ References

Ambassade de la Republique de Coree a Rabat, *Maroc-Coree: Freres de Sang*, 2022.

Morocco, a country that participated in the Korean War, Sege newspaper, Search data: November 16, 2024. https://www.segye.com/newsView/20240610514344.

Overview of Korean War of 6.25, National Archives of Korea, Search data November 15, 2024. Participation of 16 countries and the course of the war, National Archives of Korea, Search data November 15, 2024.

United Nations Veterans Act (2023), Law on Honoring UN Veterans, Law 19228, 2023.3.4. http://www.seoulcity.co.kr, Search data Nov. 13, 2024.

https://www.busan.com/view/busan/view.php?code=2022111618260528536, search data November 11, 2024.

Chapter 11

Cooperation of Aerospace Industry between Korea and Morocco

Hongje Cho (Soongsil University)

✉ chj3050@naver.com

Dr. Hongje Cho is lecturer in law at Soongsil University, where he has worked since 2023. After he had finished Ph.D. degree in international law at the University of Kyungbook in 2001, he has served as an air force officer and researched at the Korea National Defense University (KNDU) for last twenty-nine years. While doing his Ph.D. degree, he majored International Law and International Relations. He researched at KNDU on North Korea Ballistic Missile, International Space Law and Nuclear issue, International Terrorism, Nuclear Summit Meeting, North Korea Space Launch and Capability, North Korea's UAV attack, North Korea's GPS Jamming, International law and legitimacy of Preemptive Strike on North Korea Nuclear facility. Also he researched as a visiting scholar at McGill University(Canada) from Dec 2012 to May 2013 and he joined as a visiting scholar at Elliott School of International Affairs at George Washington University from Dec 2017 to Jun 2018.

I. Introduction

Compared to other African countries, Morocco, which has a relatively developed manufacturing industry, has developed a parts industry centered on the automobile and aviation industries. Morocco, which is transforming into a major producer of cutting-edge high value-added sectors, is joining the global value chain and emerging as a leader in the African economy (Cho, 2021). Accordingly, Korea's cutting-edge aerospace technology, especially satellite technology and commercial aircraft technology, is very suitable for supporting Morocco's economic growth. Aerospace cooperation with Korea has significant potential for Morocco's future growth. In this context, Morocco is making active efforts to attract Korean investors in order to bridge the gap in the global 'value chain' in the aerospace industry (Souad-anouar, 2022).

Korean investors are also increasingly attracted to Africa's vast potential (CNBC Africa, 2024). In particular, Korea is looking for ways to cooperate with Morocco, which is actively pursuing open policies and attracting foreign investors. Recent discussions between the two countries have focused on expanding bilateral economic cooperation, including the possibility of starting negotiations on an Economic Partnership Agreement (EPA). This agreement aims to expand investment and business exchanges and provide a solid legal framework for trade and investment (Kang, 2024). At the "Morocco Now" investment roadshow held in Seoul in November 2024, Moroccan officials invited Korean companies to explore opportunities in sectors such as automotive, aerospace, and renewable energy. They highlighted incentives for foreign investors in Morocco, including tax exemptions, simplified investment procedures, and personnel training programs (Korea herald, 2024). As a result of this cooperation between the two countries, Hyundai Rotem won the largest-ever electric train project worth $1.54 billion in Morocco in February 2025 (Mun, 2025).

Future cooperation plans could include joint projects in innovative areas such as aerospace manufacturing, research and development, and urban air mobility. The two countries are also considering agreements and memorandums of understanding aimed at technology transfer, personnel training, and expansion of the aerospace supply chain. Morocco's recent MOU with Brazil's Embraer to explore joint projects in commercial aviation, defense, and urban air mobility demonstrates a strong commitment to advancing the aerospace sector (Marrakesh, 2024).

In addition, Korea and Morocco signed a separate agreement on the

Economic Development Cooperation Fund (EDCF) program in June 2024, laying the legal foundation (Oh, 2024). Korea is supporting joint projects with Morocco through EDCF and expanding cooperation in the areas of transportation, energy, and green growth. This multifaceted approach provides a strong foundation for the two countries to become important partners in the aerospace industry. Therefore, this study aims to explore the possibility of cooperation in the aerospace field between Morocco and Korea and to propose future-oriented cooperation plans.

II. Status of aerospace industry in Korea and Morocco

Morocco's aerospace industry is a key economic driver and leader in Africa. Along with the automobile industry, Morocco's aerospace industry has grown the fastest to become an industry with international competitiveness. In particular, Morocco is specialized in aircraft maintenance and spare parts production, making it an investment destination of interest to Korean companies with advanced aerospace industries. Therefore, this chapter will examine the current status of the aerospace industries in Morocco and Korea and explore areas in which the two countries can cooperate in the future.

1. Status of aerospace industry in Morocco

The aerospace industry in Morocco has experienced significant growth and has established itself as a key player both domestically and internationally. The Moroccan government has identified the aerospace sector as a key driver of economic development and has strengthened its competitiveness through international cooperation and significant investments. As a result, in 2020, Morocco's aerospace industry ranked 36th in the world and 3rd in the Middle East and Africa region.

Key figures

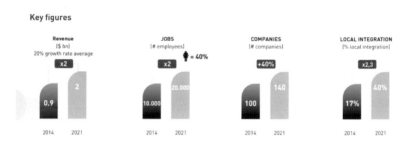

Source: file:///C:/Users/Administrator/Desktop/Pitch-Aeronautics-AMDIE%20(1).pdf

1.1. Key Sectors in Aerospace

1.1.1. Manufacturing of aircraft components

Morocco has become an important hub for manufacturing aircraft components, working with global aerospace giants such as Boeing, Airbus, Bombardier, and Safran. The country specializes in producing parts for major aircraft manufacturers, including aircraft body components, engine parts, and mechanical equipment. According to recent data, Morocco's aviation ecosystem consists of about 142 companies, generating exports of about $2 billion and providing jobs to 17,000 individuals, 40% of whom are women (The International Trade Administration, 2024). Over the past 20 years, Morocco has made significant progress in the aviation sector. As a result, it has strengthened its ambition to assemble complete aircraft domestically and has become the largest exporter of aircraft equipment in Africa. This is due to its ability to produce more than 40 major aircraft components and sensitive components manufactured in five countries around the world (Icaza, 2025).

1.1.2. Space technology

Morocco has made significant progress in space exploration and satellite technology. The country launched its first high-resolution Earth observation satellite, Mohamed VI-A, in 2017, and Mohamed VI-B in 2018. These satellites are used for both military and civilian purposes, enhancing the country's Earth monitoring capabilities. The Mohamed VI satellites are a series of two Moroccan Earth observation and reconnaissance satellites, Mohamed VI-A and Mohamed VI-B, developed and built by Airbus Defence and Space and Thales Alenia Space, based on the Astrosat-1000 satellite bus. These satellites are Morocco's first optical imaging satellites, operated by the Moroccan Ministry of Defense, and have an expected service life of five years. The satellites are named after King Mohamed VI of Morocco (Clark, 2018).

1.1.3. Defense Industry

Morocco is working hard to build a strong defense industry to consolidate its position as a regional power, meet local demand and export to foreign markets. Following the approval of the Council of Ministers for four projects related to the military sector in June 2024, the country announced its intention to create two industrial parks in the defense sector to deal with equipment, mechanisms and security weapon systems (Arredondas, 2024). The decision of the Moroccan authorities to create and establish a strong military industry stems from its desire to integrate into the regional powerhouse. Morocco has extensive experience in the automotive and aircraft manufacturing sectors and has civilian capabilities that can be transferred to the military sector. Morocco also felt the need to manufacture weapons such as drones and decided to establish a drone production plant for self-sufficiency and export. Morocco's defense sector focuses on the development and modernization of military aircraft and missile systems, incorporating aerospace technology.

The Royal Moroccan Air Force (RMAF) maintains a diverse and modern fleet of aircraft, reflecting its commitment to maintaining a strong air force capability. The core of the RMAF's fighter fleet is the F-16 Fighting Falcon acquired from the United States. The F-16 provides the RMAF with a powerful air superiority capability, equipped with advanced radars, weapon systems and electronic warfare capabilities. The RMAF also operates the French-built Mirage F1 fighter, a versatile aircraft capable of performing a variety of missions including air defense, ground attack and reconnaissance. The RMAF has also invested in upgrading its existing F-16 fleet and incorporating the latest avionics, weapon systems and software updates to ensure its combat effectiveness remains at the forefront of modern air power(Mykingsgate.co.za).

1.2. Key Aerospace Companies

Morocco's aerospace industry is supported by several prominent companies that partner with global manufacturers to produce critical components and systems.

1.2.1. Sogerma Maroc Aviation

A subsidiary of the French aerospace company EADS Sogerma is an aerospace component manufacturer located in Morocco. The company specializes in the design and manufacture of aircraft structures and cabin interior components, and produces cockpits and premium class passenger seats for commercial and military aircraft, business jets, and helicopters. Sogerma Maroc Aviation is a low-cost manufacturing facility in Morocco, operating alongside other EADS Sogerma production facilities in Rochefort, Bordeaux, and Toulouse, France (EDAS, 2008).

1.2.2. Safran Maroc

A French aerospace company Safran Maroc operating in Morocco for over 25 years, currently employing over 4,700 people through eight subsidiaries and joint ventures (Safran-group.com). Part of the global Safran Group, it produces aircraft engine components and electronic systems for the aerospace sector. Its main activities include aircraft engine maintenance, electrical harness production, and nacelle and subassembly manufacturing. In October 2024, Safran signed a Memorandum of Understanding (MOU) with the Moroccan government to establish a new LEAP engine maintenance, repair and overhaul (MRO) facility in the Casablanca airport area (Safran-group.com).

1.2.3.Bombardier Aerospace Morocco

Following the announcement of a Memorandum of Understanding (MOU) with the Moroccan government in 2011 to establish a manufacturing facility in Morocco (Newswire.co.kr), Bombardier began producing flight control components for the CRJ series regional jets in 2013 at a temporary site near Mohammed V Airport near Casablanca, employing 19 local employees. In June 2024, Bombardier met with Ryad Mezzour, Morocco's Minister of Industry, to discuss several key projects, including its participation in a project to build a fully indigenous aircraft in Morocco by 2030(Africaintelligence.com).

1.2.4. Figeac Aero

Figeac Aero is an aerospace industry specialist company founded in 1989 in Figeac, France by Jean-Claude Maillard (Figeac-aero.com). The company specializes in the manufacture of aircraft structural components, engine components, precision components and sub-assemblies, supplying products to major aircraft manufacturers worldwide. Figeac Aero is strengthening its position in the aerospace industry through continuous global expansion, establishing production facilities in various regions to provide customers with high-quality components and services.

1.3. International Collaboration

Morocco actively collaborates with international partners to foster growth in the aerospace sector. The country has established partnerships with aerospace giants such as Boeing, Airbus, Bombardier, and Safran, which have set up manufacturing and servicing facilities in Morocco. These collaborations have been instrumental in integrating Morocco into the global aerospace supply chain (Danino, 2023).

1.4. Government Support and Policies

The Moroccan government views the aerospace industry as a vital sector for economic growth and has implemented various policies to support its development. Initiatives include creating aerospace industrial clusters, such as the Midparc Free Zone near Casablanca, promoting foreign investment, and fostering technology transfer. The government has also invested in infrastructure and specialized training programs to ensure a skilled workforce for the industry (International Trade Administration, 2024).

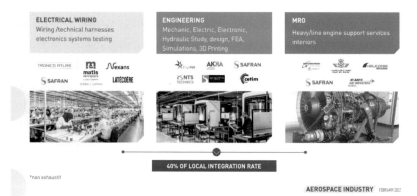

1.5. Future Outlook

The future of Morocco's aerospace industry appears promising, with continued growth expected in areas like aircraft component manufacturing, space exploration, and defense technology. The country aims to double employment in the sector by 2030 and has set an ambitious goal to manufacture a complete aircraft domestically before that year. Additionally, Morocco is exploring emerging sectors such as space tourism and commercial satellite services, positioning itself as a forward-thinking player in the aerospace industry (Huffingtonpost, 2025).

As Morocco continues to invest in aerospace research and international collaborations, it is poised to secure a more prominent position in the global aerospace market. The country's expanding capabilities, combined with its strategic initiatives, will likely allow it to further enhance its role in the international aerospace sector.

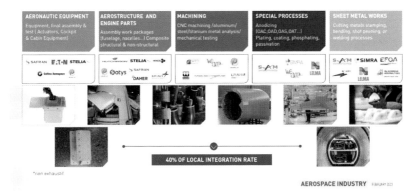

2.2. Status of aerospace industry in South Korea

The aerospace and defense market in South Korea refers to the industry in South Korea that develops, manufactures, and distributes aerospace and defense-related products and services. Included are military aircraft, satellites, defense electronics, communication systems, radar systems, and other products. R&D activities aimed at improving South Korea's capabilities in the aerospace and defense domains are also included in the market. The aerospace and defense industry in South Korea has established itself as a major player in the global aerospace and defense industry. Due to a rich history of technological advancements and a strong commitment to innovation, South Korea has positioned itself as a key market for aerospace and defense products and services. South Korea's aerospace and defense sector has expanded significantly in recent years as a result of increased defense spending, technological advancements, and collaborations with international players. The South Korea Aerospace and Defense Market Size is Expected to Hold a Significant Share by 2033, at a Compound Annual Growth Rate (CAGR) of 6.89% during the forecast period 2023 to 2033 (Sphericalinsights.com).

2.2.1. Key Companies

2.2.1.1. Korea Aerospace Industries (KAI)

As South Korea's leading aerospace manufacturer, KAI specializes in both military and civilian aircraft, as well as space development projects. Notable developments include the KT-1 basic trainer, T-50 advanced jet trainer, FA-50 light combat aircraft, and the KUH-1 utility helicopter. KAI is also involved in space programs, such as the Korea Space Launch Vehicle (Koreaaero.com).

2.2.1.2. Hanwha Aerospace

Specializing in aircraft engines, space system components, and defense equipment, Hanwha Aerospace is South Korea's sole aircraft engine producer. The company collaborates with global aviation engine companies for component manufacturing and has expanded into space-related projects (Hanwha.com).

2.2.1.3. LIG Nex1

A major defense and aerospace company, LIG Nex1 develops and produces a wide range of advanced precision electronic systems, including missiles, underwater weapon systems, radars, electronic warfare, avionics, tactical communication systems, fire control systems, naval combat systems, and electro-optics.

2.2.1.4. Korean Air Aerospace Division

Beyond its commercial airline operations, Korean Air is involved in aerospace manufacturing, including aircraft maintenance and the production of aerospace components. The company also contributes to space exploration projects.

2.2.2. Key Organizations

2.2.2.1. Korea Aerospace Research Institute (KARI)

Korea Aerospace Research Institute (KARI) is a government-funded research institute responsible for the development of aerospace technology in Korea. It was established in 1989. KARI conducts research and development in the fields of space launch vehicles, satellites, manned and unmanned aircraft, and space exploration. KARI leads the development of aerospace technology in Korea and plays a key role in fostering future space exploration and the aerospace industry (KARI.re.kr).

2.2.3. Space Industry

2.2.3.1. Nuri Rocket

South Korea's indigenous space launch vehicle, known as the Nuri rocket, represents a significant milestone in the country's space exploration capabilities. The successful launch of the Nuri rocket in 2021 marked South Korea's entry into the group of nations capable of deploying their own satellites using domestically developed technology.

2.2.3.2. Satellite Development

South Korea has been actively developing its own satellites for Earth observation, communications, and military purposes. These satellites enhance the country's capacity in space-based technologies.

2.2.4. Defense and Aerospace Integration

South Korea's aerospace sector is closely linked to its defense industry, focusing on the development of military aircraft and missile systems. Notable projects include the KF-21 Boramae, a next-generation indigenous fighter jet, and the FA-50 light combat aircraft, both of which play crucial roles in national defense.

2.2.5. Technological Innovation

The country has made significant strides in developing drones, unmanned aerial systems (UAS), and aircraft engines. Ongoing research into artificial intelligence (AI) and big data analytics aims to improve the efficiency of aerospace systems, such as aircraft performance optimization and space-based data analysis.

2.2.6. Future Prospects

The South Korea Aerospace and its Defense Market size are estimated at USD 4.88 billion in 2025, and is expected to reach USD 7.64 billion by 2030, at a CAGR of 9.38% during the forecast period (2025-2030). South Korea's aerospace & defense industry is undergoing significant transformation driven by increased regional security concerns and technological advancement. The government has demonstrated a strong commitment to defense modernization, with the 2023 defense budget reaching approximately USD 47.9 billion, marking a 1.1% increase from the previous year. The country's space systems and satellite sector has emerged as a crucial focus area for technological advancement and strategic capability development. In August 2021, the Defense Acquisition Program Administration (DAPA) unveiled an ambitious roadmap involving an investment of USD 13.6 billion by 2031 to strengthen the nation's defense infrastructure capabilities in outer space. This strategic initiative encompasses the development of military reconnaissance satellites, space-based surveillance systems, and advanced communication networks (Mordorintelligence.com).

The aerospace sector has witnessed substantial progress in indigenous aircraft development and manufacturing capabilities. A notable achievement is the increasing localization of components in major aerospace programs, with domestic manufacturers now producing approximately 65% of components for key projects like the KF-21 fighter aircraft program. This growing self-reliance in aerospace engineering has been accompanied by significant investments in research and development of advanced technologies, including unmanned aerial systems, artificial intelligence integration, and sophisticated avionics systems. The industry has also seen enhanced collaboration between domestic manufacturers and international partners, facilitating technology transfer and expertise sharing in critical aerospace technologies (Mordorintelligence.com).

The aerospace industry in South Korea is not only crucial for national security but also plays a significant role in the economy and technological innovation. Continued investment in research and development is expected to ensure South Korea's competitive position in the global aerospace industry.

III. Specific cooperation measure on aerospace industry between Korea and Morocco

The aerospace industry cooperation between Korea and Morocco can be realized through various specific measures. Here are the key ways to work together.

1. Technology Transfer and Joint Research and Development (R&D)

1.1. Satellite Technology and Component Development

South Korea's significant expertise in satellite technology can assist Morocco in enhancing its capabilities in satellite development and management. Collaborative efforts can focus on manufacturing, launch systems, and navigation technologies.

Aircraft Parts Manufacturing: South Korea's globally recognized aircraft parts manufacturing technology can be shared with Morocco to bolster local production. Joint R&D initiatives can target areas such as aircraft fuselage, engine components, and electronic systems, leading to cost efficiencies and technological self-reliance.

1.2. Urban Air Mobility (UAM) and Next-Generation Aircraft Development

Both countries can engage in collaborative research to advance UAM and next-generation aircraft technologies. By combining South Korea's technological prowess with Morocco's growth potential, they can work towards developing future aircraft and commercializing innovative technologies, including drones.

1.3. Manufacturing and Component Supply Chain Collaboration

1.3.1. Aircraft Parts Production and Technical Cooperation

South Korea can transfer its advanced aircraft parts manufacturing technologies to Morocco, promoting local production. This collaboration can enhance Morocco's self-reliance in aircraft parts production and allow South Korea to expand its supply chain, strengthening global market competitiveness.

1.3.2. Supply Chain Expansion and Optimization

Joint efforts can focus on expanding and optimizing the aerospace components supply chain. South Korea can utilize Morocco as a strategic production base, while Morocco can produce high-quality parts with technical support, supplying them to the global market. Collaboration in advanced materials and precision parts can be particularly beneficial.

1.4. Education and Human Resources Training

1.4.1. Development of Specialized Education Programs

South Korea's robust educational systems and research capabilities in aerospace can be leveraged to develop curricula aimed at training Moroccan aerospace experts. Partnerships with South Korean aerospace colleges and research institutes can facilitate this knowledge transfer.

1.4.2. Employee and Technician Training

Collaborative programs can be established to enhance the skills of

Moroccan technicians and engineers. Technical training provided by South Korean aerospace companies and research institutes will be crucial for Morocco's aerospace industry to achieve technological independence.

1.4.3. Internships and Exchange Programs

Implementing internships and exchange programs for students and professionals will allow both countries to gain practical experience in each other's aerospace industries, fostering real-world skills and knowledge transfer.

1.5. Development of Urban Air Mobility (UAM)

1.5.1. Technology Development and Testing

South Korea's leading technology in the UAM sector can be utilized to drive transportation innovation in Morocco. Joint development of UAM systems and the establishment of testbeds can address urban transportation challenges in Morocco.

1.5.2. Joint R&D Projects

Collaborative research and development projects can focus on the design, manufacturing, and safety verification of UAM vehicles, accelerating the commercialization of UAM technology in both countries.

1.5.3. Infrastructure and Regulatory Framework Development

Both nations can work together to build the necessary regulatory frameworks and urban infrastructure to support UAM commercialization, with Morocco providing an adaptable environment for UAM development.

1.6. Utilization of the Economic Development Cooperation Fund (EDCF)

1.6.1. Project Financing

South Korea can support Morocco's aerospace industry projects through the EDCF, enabling both countries to jointly promote critical infrastructure and technology development. This fund has been instrumental in financing mutually agreed-upon projects, strengthening economic cooperation between the two nations (Climate Diplomacy, 2024)

1.7. Establishing Joint Research Institutes and Building Infrastructure

1.7.1. Aerospace Research Institutes

The establishment of joint laboratories can promote aerospace technology development, focusing on innovative areas such as satellites, aircraft components, and UAM.

1.7.2. Technical Training and Education Centers

Building technical training centers in Morocco with South Korea's support can educate local technicians on cutting-edge technologies, contributing to the technological independence of Morocco's aerospace industry.

1.7.3. Joint Infrastructure Development

Collaborative development of infrastructure, such as aircraft parts manufacturing plants and UAM test airfields, will contribute to the industrial growth of both countries and enhance global supply chains.

1.7.4. Industry-Academia Cooperation

Building networks between research institutes, universities, and businesses in both countries will drive technological innovation and foster talent in the aerospace sector. These cooperation measures will enable South Korea and Morocco to combine their respective strengths, further develop the aerospace industry, and strengthen their competitiveness in the global market.

IV. Conclusion

The aerospace industry cooperation between South Korea and Morocco presents a promising avenue for mutual growth and technological advancement. By leveraging South Korea's advanced aerospace technology and Morocco's strategic position and developing industrial base, both nations can achieve significant milestones in areas such as satellite technology, aircraft component manufacturing, space exploration, and urban air mobility.

In this context, Morocco has been actively seeking dynamic partnerships with South Korea in the automotive and aeronautics sectors, recognizing the need to address "missing links" in its value chains. This initiative aligns with Morocco's broader strategy to attract Korean investors and enhance its industrial capabilities. By focusing on key areas of cooperation, including technology transfer, joint research and development, manufacturing partnerships, human resource development, and infrastructure establishment, both countries can create a robust framework for long-term success.

Additionally, their participation in emerging sectors like urban air mobility and space exploration promises to lead to innovative breakthroughs that will impact the future of transportation and space industries globally. Through continued collaboration and the utilization of financial mechanisms such as the Economic Development Cooperation Fund (EDCF), South Korea and Morocco can accelerate the growth of their aerospace sectors. This partnership will not only enhance their technological capabilities but also contribute to fostering economic growth, technological independence, and international cooperation, paving the way for a prosperous aerospace future for both nations.

References

Africaintelligence.com. https://www.africaintelligence.com/north-africa/2024/06/20/ bombardier-eyes-fully-home-made-moroccan-aircraft,110249839-eve. Accessed Feb. 23, 2025.

Cho, Hwa-Rim. Morocco's economic status before the Covid-19 pandemic, *Geonji Inmunhak,* no.31, 2021: 77-103.

Clark, Stephen. Moroccan spy satellite launched aboard Vega rocket, *Spaceflightnow,* Nov. 21, 2018. ttps://spaceflightnow.com/2018/11/21/moroccan-spy-satellite-launched-aboard-vega-rocket/. Accessed Feb. 23, 2025.

Climate Diplomacy. Morocco and South Korea agree to cooperate on green transition efforts.Tuesday, Jun. 4, 2024. https://enterprise.news/climate/en/news/story/63b46383-0fc1-47a4-b715-49e2ac57e029/morocco-and-south-korea-agree-to-cooperate-on-green-transition-efforts. Accessed Feb. 23, 2025.

CNBC Afria. Korean investors seek African investment opportunities, *CNBCAFRICA,* Dec. 6, 2024. https://www.cnbcafrica.com/media/6365637266112/korean-investors-seek-african-investment-opportunities/ Accessed Feb. 23, 2025.

Daniel Danino, Taking Advantage Of Morocco's Emerging Aerospace Industry, FORBES.COM. May 17, 2023. https://www.forbes.com/councils/forbesbusin esscouncil/2023/05/17/taking-advantage-of-moroccos-emerging-aerospace-industry/?utm_source.

EDAS. *Registration Document 2008.* https://www.airbus.com/sites/g/files/jlcbta136/files/2021-07/annual-report08-registration-document-business-governance-en-08-1.pdf?utm_source=chatgpt.com. Accessed Feb. 23, 2025.

EMBRAER.COM, Moroccan Government Signs Aerospace Cooperation Agreement with Embraer. 10/30/2024, https://www.embraer.com/global/en/news?slug=1207473-moroccan-government-signs-aerospace-cooperation-agreement-with-embraer&utm_source.

ENTERPRISE.NEWS, CLIMATE DIPLOMACY, Morocco and South Korea agree to cooperate on green transition efforts. Tuesday, 4 June 2024. https://enterprise. news/climate/en/news/story/63b46383-0fc1-47a4-b715-49e2ac57e029/ morocco-and-south-korea-agree-to-cooperate-on-green-transition-efforts.

Figeac-aero.com. https://www.figeac-aero.com/en/history?utm_source=chatgpt.com. Accessed Feb. 23, 2025.

HANWHA.COM, https://www.hanwha.com/companies/hanwha-aerospace.do?utm_ source=chatgpt.com.

Hanwhaaerospace.com. https://www.hanwhaaerospace.com/kor/whoweare/about.do. Accessed Feb. 23, 2025.

Huffingtonpost. Marruecos aprieta el acelerador para convertirse en el rey de los cielos, Jan. 8, 2025. https://www.huffingtonpost.es/sociedad/marruecos-aprieta-acelerador-convertirse-reycielos.html?utm_source.. Accessed Feb. 23, 2025.

HUFFINGTONPOST.ES, Marruecos aprieta el acelerador para convertirse en el rey de los cielos Marruecos lidera en África como potencia aeronáutica y aspira a fabricar un avión completo antes de 2030. Redacción HuffPost, 08/01/2025, https://www.huffingtonpost.es/sociedad/marruecos-aprieta-acelerador-convertirse-rey-cielos.html?utm_source.

Icaza, Adriana. Morocco rises to fifth place in the world in the aviation industry and leads Africa, *Atalaya,* Jan. 5, 2025. https://www.atalayar.com/en/articulo/ economy-andbusiness/%E2%80%8B-%E2%80%8B/20250105100000209466. html. Accessed Feb. 23, 2025.

International Trade Administration. Morocco-country-commercial-guides/morocco-aerospace, Jan. 1, 2024. https://www.trade.gov/country-commercial-guides/ morocco-aerospace. Accessed Feb. 23, 2025.

Kang Yoon-seung, S. Korea, Morocco discuss bilateral economic ties, potential EPA, November 28, 2024, EN.YNA.CO.KR, https://en.yna.co.kr/view/ AEN20241128001100320?utm_source.

Kari.re.kr. https://www.kari.re.kr/kor.do. Accessed Feb. 23, 2025.

Koreaaero.com. https://www.koreaaero.com/EN/Company/AboutKAI.aspx. Accessed Feb. 23, 2025.

Koreaaero.com. Morocco promises robust incentives for Korean businesses. Nov. 29, 2024. https://www.koreaherald.com/article/10012014. Accessed February 23, 2025.

KOREAHERALD.COM. Morocco promises robust incentives for Korean businesses. Nov. 29, 2024, https://www.koreaherald.com/article/10012014.

M.KOREAAERO.COM, https://m.koreaaero.com/EN/Company/AboutKAI. aspx?utm_source.

Margarita, Arredondas. Morocco is strengthening its defence industry in order to consolidate its position as a regional power, Atalayar, Nov. 5, 2024. https://www.atalayar.com/en/articulo/politics/morocco-is-strengthening-its-defence-industry-in-order-to-consolidate-its-position-regional-ower/20241105190000207327.html. Accessed Feb. 23, 2025.

Marrakesh. Moroccan Government Signs Aerospace Cooperation Agreement with Embraer, *embraer.com*, Oct. 30, 2024. https://www.embraer.com/global/en/news?slug=1207473-moroccan-government-signs-aerospace-cooperation-agreement-with-embraer. Accessed Feb. 23, 2025.

MINM.MA.Morocco's Aerospace Industry: A Key Global Manufacturing Hub° https://minm.ma/aerospace-aviation/the-moroccan-aerospace-industry-a-strategic-hub-for-global-manufacturing/?utm_source.

Mordorintelligence.com. https://www.mordorintelligence.com/industry-\reports/south-korea-aerospace-and-defense-market. Accessed Feb. 23, 2025.

MOROCCOWORLDNEWS.COM. https://www.moroccoworldnews.com/2022/07/350219/morocco-seeks-dynamic-partnership-with-korea-in-auto-aeronautics-sectors?utm_source.

Mun, Su bin. Hyundai Rotem secures record 2.2 trillion won electric train order from

Morocco, Feb. 26, 2025. https://www.koreaherald.com/article/10428849 Accessed Feb. 26, 2025.

Mykingsgate.co.za. https://mykingsgate.co.za/info/morocco-air-force-42622/. Accessed Feb. 23, 2025.

Oh, Seok-min. Korea, Morocco discuss joint economic projects on energy, transport, *Yonhap News,* Sep. 25, 2024. https://en.yna.co.kr/view/AEN20240925002400320. Accessed Feb. 23, 2025.

S. Korea, Morocco discuss bilateral economic ties, potential EPA | Yonhap News Agency (yna.co.kr)

Safran-group.com. https://www.safran-group.com/countries/morocco?utm_source=chatgpt.com. Accessed Feb. 23, 2025.

Souad-anouar. Morocco Seeks 'Dynamic' Partnership with Korea in Auto, Aeronautics Sectors, *Morocco world news,* Jul. 12, 2022. https://www.moroccoworldnews.com/2022/07/43769/morocco-seeks-dynamic-partnership-with-korea-in-auto-aeronautics-sectors/ Accessed Feb. 23, 2025.

Souad Anouar, Morocco Seeks 'Dynamic' Partnership with Korea in Auto, Aeronautics Sectors With Morocco and Korea celebrating 60 years of diplomatic relations this year, Rabat seeks to further attract Korean investors to advance its local industries. July 12, 2022, MOROCCOWORLDNEWS.COM.

Sphericalinsights.com. https://www.sphericalinsights.com/reports/south-korea-aerospace-and-defense-market. Accessed Feb. 23, 2025.

TRADE.GOV. Morocco - Country Commercial Guide° https://www.trade.gov/country-commercial-guides/morocco-aerospace?utm_source.

TRADE.GOV. Official Website of the International Trade Administration, Here's how you know, Morocco-CountryCommercial Guide. https://www.trade.gov/country-commercial-guides/morocco-aerospace?utm_source.

Chapter 12

Korea-Morocco collaboration in Supercapacitor technology for Sustainable Energy

N. S. Reddy (Gyeongsang National University)

✉ nsreddy@gnu.ac.kr

Dr. Nagireddy Gari Subba Reddy (N. S. Reddy) is a Full Professor of Materials Science at Gyeongsang National University (GNU), Jinju, South Korea. He holds a Ph.D. in Computational Materials Science from IIT Kharagpur, India, along with degrees in Metallurgy, Mechanical Engineering, and diploma in Automobile Engineering. With nearly 90 Q1 and Q2 publications, he actively mentors students in research and thesis writing. His expertise spans Artificial Neural Networks (ANN), Explainable AI (XAI), and Machine Learning (ML), applied to high-entropy alloys, battery materials, diffusion prediction, corrosion modeling, sustainability, and healthcare. He has developed ANN-based sustainability analysis software, integrating prediction, sensitivity analysis, and variable optimization. His recent work extends ANN and XAI to entrepreneurial marketing and social sciences. His current projects include sustainability modeling in nonprofit healthcare, AI-driven energy materials, creep rupture life prediction in steels, and Titanium alloy microstructure-property relationships. Actively collaborating across disciplines, he contributes to AI-driven materials research and industrial applications. Dr. Reddy has built a strong global research network through collaborations and academic visits to Hong Kong, Thailand, Malaysia, Taiwan, Singapore, Czech Republic, Germany, the UK, the US, and Japan, advancing AI, materials science, and sustainability.

I. Introduction

Energy storage technology plays a crucial role in the transition toward renewable energy sources. Supercapacitors, with their high power density, rapid charge-discharge cycles, and long lifecycle, are emerging as a viable solution to enhance energy storage capacity. Korea has positioned itself as a leader in supercapacitor research and industrial production, making advancements in electrode materials, electrolyte composition, and scalable manufacturing techniques. Meanwhile, Morocco, with its abundant natural resources, has the potential to contribute to the global supercapacitor market by providing essential raw materials for supercapacitor components. This paper explores the collaborative potential between Korea and Morocco in supercapacitor technology, emphasizing knowledge exchange, resource utilization, and technology transfer.

1. Introduction to Supercapacitors

Supercapacitors, also known as ultracapacitors or electrochemical capacitors, are advanced energy storage devices that bridge the gap between conventional capacitors and batteries. Unlike batteries, which store energy through chemical reactions, supercapacitors store energy electrostatically. This allows them to charge and discharge at significantly higher rates, making them highly efficient for applications that require rapid energy delivery, such as regenerative braking in electric vehicles and power stabilization in renewable energy systems (Conway, 1999) Supercapacitors consist of two electrodes separated by an electrolyte, where energy is stored at the interface of the electrode material and electrolyte in the electric double layer. In addition to electric double-layer capacitance (EDLC), some supercapacitors also exhibit pseudocapacitance, a charge storage mechanism that involves fast, reversible electrochemical reactions at the electrode surface. Pseudocapacitance enhances energy density beyond that of traditional capacitors, allowing supercapacitors to store more energy without compromising their high power output (Brousse et al., 2015; Burke, 2000).

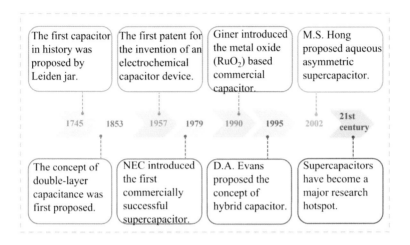

Figure 1. Development history of Supercapacitors (Yang et al., 2023).

The timeline illustrates (Figure 1) the key historical milestones in the development of capacitors and supercapacitors, starting from the proposal of the first capacitor, the Leiden jar, in 1745. In 1853, the concept of double-layer capacitance was first introduced, paving the way for electrochemical capacitor advancements. The first patent for an electrochemical capacitor was filed in 1957, followed by NEC's introduction of the first commercially successful supercapacitor in 1979. In 1990, Giner developed a commercial capacitor based on metal oxide (RuO₂), and in 1995, D.A. Evans proposed the concept of hybrid capacitors. In 2002, M.S. Hong introduced the aqueous asymmetric supercapacitor, further expanding research in the field. Entering the 21st century, supercapacitors have become a significant research focus, contributing to advancements in energy storage technologies.

2. Classification of Supercapacitors

Supercapacitors are broadly classified into three main types based on their charge storage mechanisms, as illustrated in **Figure 1**: electrochemical double-layer capacitors (EDLCs), **pseudocapacitors, and hybrid supercapacitors.**

1) **Electric Double-Layer Capacitors** (EDLCs) store energy electrostatically without involving chemical reactions. They utilize high-surface-area carbon-based materials such as **activated carbon, aerogel, nanoscaled allotropes of carbon, and graphene** to maximize charge storage. EDLCs are known for their long cycle life and rapid charge/discharge capability, making them ideal for applications requiring high power density.

2) **Pseudocapacitors** store charge through reversible faradaic reactions occurring at the electrode surface. These capacitors incorporate **redox-active materials** such as **redox polymers, redox metal oxides** (e.g., RuO_2, MnO_2), **and soluble redox electrolytes** to enhance capacitance. Pseudocapacitors provide higher energy density compared to EDLCs but exhibit lower stability due to the continuous involvement of redox reactions *(Brousse et al., 2015)*.

3) **Hybrid Supercapacitors** integrate the advantages of both EDLCs and pseudocapacitors by combining different electrode materials to achieve an optimal balance between energy density and power density. These include **composite electrodes, EDLC/pseudocapacitor hybrids, and battery/supercapacitor hybrids.** Examples of hybrid supercapacitors include lithium-ion capacitors *(LICs)* and asymmetric supercapacitors, which utilize a **battery-like anode** and a **capacitor-like cathode** to

optimize performance *(Simon & Gogotsi, 2008)*. The classification of supercapacitors is depicted in **Figure 1**, categorizing them into EDLCs, pseudocapacitors, and hybrid capacitors along with their respective material compositions.

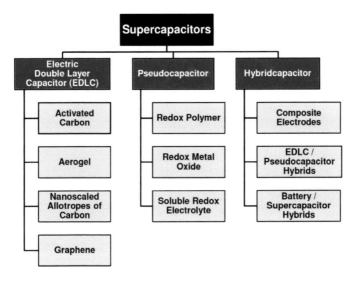

Figure 2. Classification diagram of Supercapacitors

3. Importance of Supercapacitors for Energy Storage

Supercapacitors play an essential role in modern energy storage applications due to their unique advantages. Their high power density enables rapid charge and discharge cycles, making them ideal for applications such as load balancing in power grids and kinetic energy recovery in electric vehicles *(Burke, 2000)*. Unlike conventional batteries, supercapacitors have an exceptionally long cycle life, capable of enduring millions of charge-discharge cycles without significant degradation, making them a durable and reliable energy storage solution (Simon & Gogotsi, 2008). Furthermore, supercapacitors function efficiently over a wide range of temperatures, making them suitable for industrial, aerospace, and extreme environmental applications (Zhang & Zhao, 2009). Additionally, by incorporating environmental friendly electrode materials, supercapacitors contribute to sustainable energy solutions and reduce the ecological impact of energy storage systems (Brousse et al., 2015).

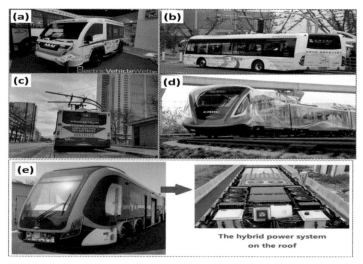

Figure 3. Various applications of supercapacitors in electric vehicles: (a) Tata Magic Hybrid vehicle. Reproduced from https://electricvehicleweb.com/arai-tata-magic-hybrid-vehicle-isro/. (b) Capabus recharging at the bus stop. Reproduced from, https://handwiki.org/wiki/index.php?title=Engineering:Capa_vehicle&oldid=2536027. (c) SmartBUS in Turin using supercapacitors. Reproduced from https://www.sustainable-bus.com/electric-bus/smartbus-turin-supercapacitors/. (d) Chinese rail giant CRRC has debuted its first hydrogen-powered passenger train using supercapacitors. Reproduced from https://newatlas.com/transport/china-hydrogen-supercapacitor-train/.

4. Emerging Research in Supercapacitor Technology

The evolution of supercapacitors faces several key challenges that hinder their widespread application, including material stability, fast discharging, narrow potential windows, redox activity restrictions, and internal resistance. However, recent advancements in nanotechnology and material science are addressing these limitations, significantly enhancing supercapacitor performance. Researchers are exploring graphene-based electrodes, which provide exceptional electrical conductivity and a large surface area, increasing charge storage capacity(Zhang & Zhao, 2009). Additionally, heteroatom-doped carbons, where elements such as nitrogen, sulfur, and oxygen are introduced into carbon materials, have demonstrated improved charge storage capability and electrochemical stability, further boosting supercapacitor efficiency (Brousse et al., 2015).

To overcome existing challenges, future solutions include template-free synthesis for scalable and cost-effective production of electrode materials, multi-material inclusion to enhance synergistic charge storage mechanisms, and hybrid device integration, combining supercapacitors with batteries for improved performance. The development of ionic liquid electrolytes has further enhanced voltage stability and ionic conductivity, leading to improvements in energy density and device longevity. Additionally, material cooperative integrity and the design of novel nanomaterials are paving the way for supercapacitors with higher energy density, better cycle stability, and wider operating voltage windows.

As supercapacitors continue to evolve, they are expected to play a critical role in the global transition toward sustainable energy solutions. Their ability to complement and enhance battery performance makes them a key component in next-generation energy storage systems. Furthermore, international collaborations, such as those between Korea and Morocco, can drive further advancements by integrating technological expertise with natural resource availability, accelerating the development of more efficient and sustainable supercapacitor technologies. The figure 4 highlights key challenges in supercapacitors, such as material stability, fast discharging, and internal resistance, alongside future solutions like template-free synthesis, multi-material inclusion, and hybrid integration. These advancements aim to enhance energy density, stability, and efficiency, driving supercapacitors toward broader adoption in energy storage.

Figure 4. Schematic of several current challenges and future solutions to obtaining highly applicable supercapacitor devices (Kumar et al., 2022).

II. Korea's Leadership in Supercapacitor Technology

Korea has made significant strides in supercapacitor technology, particularly in material development, nanotechnology applications, and scalable production processes. Korean researchers and companies have focused on enhancing energy density, improving charge-discharge rates, and increasing longevity, making supercapacitors more viable for applications such as:

- **Renewable Energy Storage**: Supercapacitors help stabilize power grids by storing excess energy generated from renewable sources such as solar and wind energy, reducing reliance on fossil fuels. Recent advances in supercapacitor-based energy storage systems have shown improvements in power density and operational lifespan, making them an integral part of Korea's green energy initiatives *(Yadlapalli et al., 2022).*

- **Electric Vehicles** (EVs)*:* Supercapacitors provide rapid energy bursts for acceleration and braking energy recovery, enhancing the efficiency of electric vehicles. Korean automakers and battery manufacturers, including Hyundai and Samsung SDI, have been integrating supercapacitors into hybrid and electric vehicles to improve energy efficiency and performance.

- **Portable Electronics***:* The demand for compact and efficient energy storage solutions in consumer electronics has led Korean researchers to develop high-performance micro-supercapacitors. These innovations have significantly extended the battery life of wearables and smartphones by providing quick power boosts.

- **Grid Stabilization***:* Supercapacitors play a crucial role in maintaining grid stability by rapidly compensating for fluctuations in power supply and demand. Korea has implemented smart grid projects utilizing supercapacitor-based storage systems to enhance grid resilience and efficiency *(Yadlapalli et al., 2022).*

Major Korean companies and research institutions have invested heavily in R&D, ensuring that supercapacitors continue to evolve as an effective energy storage solution. Leading institutions such as KAIST, Seoul National University, and POSTECH have pioneered advancements in supercapacitor electrode materials, including graphene-based and heteroatom-doped carbon materials (Wu, 2023). Additionally, companies like LG Chem and SK Innovation have been actively developing next-generation supercapacitors with enhanced energy density and cycle stability (Olabi et al., 2022).

Government policies and funding have also played a crucial role in fostering innovation within this sector. The Korean government has provided significant research grants and incentives to support supercapacitor research as part of its broader strategy to achieve carbon neutrality by 2050. National projects such as the Green Energy Innovation Program and partnerships with international research bodies have further accelerated the commercialization of advanced supercapacitor technologies.

III. Morocco's Potential in Supercapacitor Development

Morocco is in the early stages of supercapacitor research and development but possesses significant natural advantages. These strengths make it a promising location for future supercapacitor innovations and collaborations. Key advantages include:

- **Abundant Natural Resources**: Morocco has rich deposits of essential minerals such as phosphate, carbon precursors, and transition metals, which are vital for the production of supercapacitor electrodes and electrolytes. Activated carbon derived from Moroccan biomass and mineral resources like vanadium, manganese, and cobalt could be utilized to develop cost-effective and high-performance energy storage materials.
- **Renewable Energy Leadership**: Morocco has one of the most ambitious

renewable energy programs in Africa, with large-scale investments in solar and wind power, such as the Noor Ouarzazate Solar Complex, one of the largest concentrated solar power plants in the world. Supercapacitors can play a critical role in these renewable energy projects by providing rapid charge and discharge capabilities, improving grid stability, and enabling better energy management in off-grid and microgrid applications (Boulakhbar et al., 2020).

- **Growing Research and Development Infrastructure:** Moroccan universities and research institutions are expanding their focus on energy storage technologies. Institutions like Mohammed VI Polytechnic University (UM6P) and Cadi Ayyad University have initiated research projects on advanced materials, energy storage solutions, and nanotechnology applications. Government-backed initiatives and funding programs aimed at fostering research in clean energy and sustainable materials further enhance Morocco's potential to become a key player in the supercapacitor industry (Choukri et al., 2017).

- **Strategic Location for Global Trade:** Morocco's geographic position provides an excellent gateway to European, African, and Middle Eastern markets, facilitating collaboration and trade in energy storage materials and technologies. This makes Morocco an attractive hub for industrial-scale production and export of supercapacitor components (Sakhraoui et al., 2024).

Given these factors, Morocco is well-positioned to leverage its resources and growing expertise to collaborate with Korea in supercapacitor technology development. Collaborative efforts could involve knowledge transfer, joint research projects, and industrial partnerships aimed at scaling up supercapacitor production for sustainable energy applications.

IV. Opportunities for Korea-Morocco Collaboration

A strategic partnership between Korea and Morocco can bring numerous benefits to both countries. This collaboration can leverage Korea's expertise in advanced energy storage technologies and Morocco's rich natural resources, contributing to the development of cost-effective and high-performance supercapacitor solutions. The key areas of collaboration include:

1. Knowledge Exchange and Capacity Building

- **Expertise Sharing:** Korean researchers and engineers can share their knowledge in nanotechnology, material synthesis, and supercapacitor fabrication techniques. Leading institutions such as KAIST, POSTECH, and Seoul National University have pioneered research in energy storage materials, making their expertise invaluable in this collaboration (Horn et al., 2019).
- **Training Programs and Research Collaboration:** Moroccan scientists and engineers can receive specialized training and collaborate on joint research projects, helping to develop local expertise in supercapacitor technology. This could involve exchange programs, internships, and workshops hosted by Korean universities and research centers.
- **Establishment of Research Centers:** Setting up joint research centers in Morocco focusing on energy storage can foster continuous collaboration

and innovation. These centers can facilitate knowledge transfer and promote long-term sustainability in supercapacitor development.

2. Joint Research and Development Projects

- **Development of Cost-Effective Electrode Materials:** Moroccan resources, such as biomass-derived carbon and mineral-based electrolytes, can be utilized to develop cost-effective supercapacitor electrodes. Studies have shown that activated carbon derived from biomass can significantly enhance the performance of supercapacitors due to its high surface area and conductivity.
- **Hybrid Energy Storage Systems:** Research can focus on integrating supercapacitors with batteries to enhance the efficiency and lifespan of energy storage systems. Hybrid systems that combine supercapacitors with lithium-ion batteries have been found to optimize energy density while maintaining high power output.
- **Sustainable and Scalable Production Methods:** Investigating environmentally friendly manufacturing techniques, such as green synthesis of electrode materials and the use of non-toxic electrolytes, can contribute to sustainable supercapacitor production. This research aligns with global efforts to minimize the carbon footprint of energy storage technologies.

3. Technology Transfer and Industrial Partnerships

- **Establishing Pilot Production Facilities:** Korean companies, with their extensive experience in supercapacitor manufacturing, can establish partnerships with Moroccan firms to set up pilot production facilities. This will not only reduce production costs but also create employment opportunities and boost local expertise.

- **Joint Ventures for Local Manufacturing and Assembly:** Encouraging collaborations between Korean and Moroccan industries can lead to the development of local manufacturing units for supercapacitor components. This can help reduce import dependency and promote technological self-reliance in Morocco.
- **Integration into Global Supply Chains:** Morocco's strategic geographic position makes it an ideal location for exporting supercapacitor components to Europe, Africa, and the Middle East. Establishing strong supply chain networks can enhance Morocco's participation in the global energy storage market.

By leveraging Korea's technological advancements and Morocco's natural resource potential, this collaboration can play a crucial role in shaping the future of sustainable energy storage. The successful implementation of these initiatives will not only benefit both nations economically but also contribute to global energy sustainability efforts.

V. Expected Benefits of Collaboration

1. Advancing Sustainable Energy Solutions

- **Development of Efficient and Eco-Friendly Energy Storage Systems:** The Korea-Morocco collaboration can lead to the creation of more efficient and environmentally friendly energy storage solutions, supporting Morocco's renewable energy goals while leveraging Korea's technological expertise. Advanced supercapacitor technology can enhance the sustainability of renewable energy projects by enabling efficient energy capture, storage, and utilization

- **Enhancing Renewable Energy Integration:** Supercapacitors are known for their ability to provide rapid charge and discharge capabilities, making them ideal for enhancing the reliability of intermittent renewable energy sources such as solar and wind power. By integrating supercapacitors into Morocco's renewable energy infrastructure, energy storage efficiency can be improved, leading to greater stability in electricity supply and reduced dependency on fossil fuels

- **Reducing Carbon Footprint:** The adoption of advanced supercapacitors can help reduce greenhouse gas emissions by facilitating the transition from conventional fossil-fuel-based energy sources to sustainable alternatives. Korea's research and development in green energy storage solutions can aid Morocco in achieving its carbon neutrality targets.

2. Economic and Industrial Growth

- **Utilization of Morocco's Natural Resources for Economic Gain:** Morocco's rich deposits of essential minerals and carbon-based materials can be utilized to develop cost-effective supercapacitor components. This can create new industries centered on material extraction, processing, and electrode fabrication, boosting Morocco's economy and creating job opportunities.

- **Expansion of Market Opportunities for Korean Companies:** By investing in Moroccan energy storage projects, Korean companies can benefit from access to new markets in Africa and Europe. Morocco's strategic location offers opportunities for exporting supercapacitor-based energy storage solutions to regions with growing renewable energy demands.

• **Development of Local Manufacturing Infrastructure:** Establishing joint manufacturing units in Morocco will reduce import dependency and encourage local production of supercapacitor components. This will foster industrial growth while making supercapacitor technology more accessible to African markets.

3. Strengthening Bilateral Relations

• **Model for Future Scientific and Industrial Partnerships:** A successful collaboration in supercapacitor technology can serve as a blueprint for other scientific and industrial partnerships between Korea and Morocco. It can also inspire similar collaborations between other countries looking to enhance their clean energy capabilities.

• **Expansion into Other High-Tech Sectors:** The success of the Korea-Morocco partnership in energy storage may encourage further collaborations in related fields such as electric mobility, smart grid technologies, and advanced nanomaterials. By leveraging each country's strengths, future initiatives can explore new frontiers in green technology.

• **Strengthening Diplomatic and Economic Ties:** This collaboration can contribute to stronger diplomatic relations between Korea and Morocco, fostering long-term cooperation in technology transfer, research collaboration, and industrial investment. It can also enhance economic ties by facilitating trade agreements related to energy storage materials and technologies.

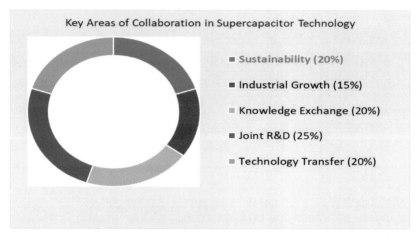

Key Areas of Collaboration in Supercapacitor Technology

- Sustainability (20%)
- Industrial Growth (15%)
- Knowledge Exchange (20%)
- Joint R&D (25%)
- Technology Transfer (20%)

Figure 5. Key Areas of Korea-Morocco Collaboration in Supercapacitor Technology

This pie chart visually represents the **distribution of collaborative efforts** between Korea and Morocco in advancing supercapacitor technology. The five main areas of collaboration—**Knowledge Exchange, Joint R&D, Technology Transfer, Industrial Growth, and Sustainability**—are assigned proportional values based on their relative impact.

Knowledge Exchange (20%) highlights the transfer of expertise in nanotechnology, material synthesis, and supercapacitor fabrication from Korea to Morocco. **Joint Research & Development** (25%) focuses on developing cost-effective electrode materials, hybrid energy storage systems, and environmentally friendly production methods. **Technology Transfer** (20%) plays a crucial role in scaling up production, ensuring

Morocco gains access to advanced manufacturing techniques and efficient energy storage solutions.

Industrial Growth (15%) represents the potential for economic expansion, including local manufacturing of supercapacitor components and integration into global supply chains. Finally, **Sustainability** (20%) underlines the environmental benefits of this collaboration, including reducing reliance on fossil fuels and supporting Morocco's renewable energy initiatives. This visualization demonstrates how a structured **bilateral partnership** can effectively **leverage Korea's technological leadership and Morocco's resource potential**, contributing to global advancements in energy storage technology.

VI. Challenges and Considerations

While the potential benefits of a Korea-Morocco collaboration in supercapacitor technology are significant, several challenges must be addressed to ensure successful implementation and long-term sustainability.

1. Infrastructure Development

- **Need for Research Facilities and Pilot-Scale Production Units:** Morocco lacks the necessary large-scale research infrastructure for supercapacitor development. While the country has growing research institutions focusing on renewable energy, dedicated facilities for supercapacitor fabrication, testing, and scale-up production are limited.

- **Technology Transfer and Capacity Building:** To bridge the technological gap, Morocco needs substantial investment in research infrastructure, including state-of-the-art material synthesis laboratories and electrochemical testing facilities.

- **Government and Private Sector Investment:** The Moroccan government must partner with private enterprises and international research organizations to fund new research centers and pilot-scale supercapacitor production units.

2. Funding and Investment

- **Public and Private Financial Support:** Both Korean and Moroccan governments, along with private sector stakeholders, need to provide dedicated funding to support supercapacitor research and development initiatives.

- **Incentives for Foreign Direct Investment** (FDI): Morocco should establish financial incentives, such as tax benefits and subsidies, to attract foreign companies to invest in its supercapacitor industry.

- **Collaboration with International Financial Institutions:** Partnerships with the World Bank, African Development Bank, and other international funding agencies can provide financial assistance for infrastructure development and technological advancements.

3. Regulatory and Policy Alignment

- **Clear Policies for Technology Transfer:** A well-defined regulatory framework is required to facilitate technology transfer agreements between Korean and Moroccan research institutions and industries.
- **Standardization and Quality Assurance:** Supercapacitor production must comply with international standards to ensure compatibility and commercial viability in global markets.
- **Government Support for Industry Growth:** Policymakers must create regulations that promote research collaborations, facilitate international trade, and support local manufacturing of supercapacitor components.

4. Market Adoption

- **Demonstrating Commercial Viability:** The commercial success of supercapacitors depends on proving their efficiency, cost-effectiveness, and long-term reliability in various applications, such as electric vehicles, smart grids, and consumer electronics.
- **Public Awareness and Industry Engagement:** There is a need for increased awareness among policymakers, investors, and end-users about the benefits of supercapacitors as an energy storage solution.
- **Encouraging Industrial and Academic Collaboration:** Stronger ties between universities and industries can accelerate the commercialization of supercapacitor technology by fostering innovation-driven partnerships.

By addressing these challenges through targeted investments, regulatory support, and strategic collaborations, the Korea-Morocco partnership can successfully advance supercapacitor technology and contribute to sustainable energy solutions.

VII. Conclusion and Future Prospects

The collaboration between Korea and Morocco in supercapacitor technology presents a promising opportunity to advance sustainable energy storage solutions. By leveraging Korea's expertise in supercapacitor development and Morocco's abundant natural resources, both countries can foster technological innovation, economic growth, and environmental sustainability.

Korea has demonstrated global leadership in supercapacitor technology, with advanced research in nanostructured electrode materials, scalable fabrication techniques, and hybrid energy storage solutions. Meanwhile, Morocco offers rich deposits of carbon-based resources and a strong commitment to renewable energy initiatives. By combining these strengths, the two nations can co-develop cost-effective and high-performance supercapacitor systems for applications in electric vehicles, grid stabilization, and portable electronics. Moving forward, structured research initiatives, industrial partnerships, and supportive policies will be essential to realizing the full potential of this collaboration. Joint efforts in infrastructure development, knowledge exchange, and technology transfer will pave the way for a more sustainable and resilient energy future.

VIII. Recommendations

To maximize the benefits of this partnership, the following strategic steps should be undertaken:

1. Establish a Joint Research Initiative

○ Korean and Moroccan universities and research institutions should collaborate on supercapacitor development projects. This will involve knowledge-sharing programs, joint PhD research opportunities, and faculty exchange programs to enhance technical expertise.

2. Develop Pilot-Scale Production Facilities

○ With technical support from Korean companies, Morocco should establish pilot-scale production units for supercapacitor components. These facilities will help transition from laboratory-scale research to commercial-scale production, accelerating market entry and industrial adoption.

3. Encourage Government and Private Sector Investment

○ Policymakers should introduce incentives such as tax exemptions, funding grants, and public-private partnerships to attract investors in supercapacitor technology. Financial institutions like the World Bank and the African Development Bank can provide funding for large-scale infrastructure projects.

4. Facilitate Technology Transfer Agreements

○ Structured agreements between Korean and Moroccan industries should be established to ensure knowledge transfer and capacity building. This includes licensing agreements for proprietary technologies, joint ventures for production, and intellectual property protection to encourage innovation.

5. Organize Annual Korea-Morocco Energy Summits

○ Hosting an annual conference dedicated to energy storage solutions will foster stronger bilateral ties. These summits will serve as platforms for industry leaders, researchers, and policymakers to discuss advancements, challenges, and new opportunities in supercapacitor technology.

A strong Korea-Morocco partnership can drive supercapacitor innovation and sustainable energy, enhancing industrial ties, advancing clean energy goals, and promoting global energy security.

■ References

Boulakhbar, M., Lebrouhi, B., Kousksou, T., Smouh, S., Jamil, A., Maaroufi, M., & Zazi, M. (2020). Towards a large-scale integration of renewable energies in Morocco. *Journal of Energy Storage, 32*, 101806. https://doi.org/https://doi.org/10.1016/j.est.2020.101806

Brousse, T., Bélanger, D., & Long, J. W. (2015). To Be or Not To Be Pseudocapacitive. *Journal of The Electrochemical Society, 162.*

Burke, A. (2000). Ultracapacitors: why, how, and where is the technology. *Journal of Power Sources, 91*(1), 37-50. https://doi.org/https://doi.org/10.1016/S0378-7753(00)00485-7

Choukri, K., Naddami, A., & Hayani, S. (2017). Renewable energy in emergent countries: lessons from energy transition in Morocco. *Energy, Sustainability and Society, 7*(1), 25. https://doi.org/10.1186/s13705-017-0131-2

Conway, B. E. (1999). Electrochemical Supercapacitors: Scientific Fundamentals and Technological Applications.

Horn, M., MacLeod, J., Liu, M., Webb, J., & Motta, N. (2019). Supercapacitors: A new source of power for electric cars? *Economic Analysis and Policy, 61*, 93-103. https://doi.org/https://doi.org/10.1016/j.eap.2018.08.003

Kumar, N., Kim, S.-B., Lee, S.-Y., & Park, S.-J. (2022). Recent Advanced Supercapacitor: A Review of Storage Mechanisms, Electrode Materials, Modification, and Perspectives. *Nanomaterials, 12*(20), 3708. https://www.mdpi.com/2079-4991/12/20/3708

Olabi, A. G., Abbas, Q., Al Makky, A., & Abdelkareem, M. A. (2022). Supercapacitors as next generation energy storage devices: Properties and applications. *Energy, 248*, 123617. https://doi.org/https://doi.org/10.1016/j.energy.2022.123617

Sakhraoui, K., Agadi, R., von Hirschhausen, C., & Ege, G. S. (2024). Energy policy in morocco: Analysis of the national energy strategy's impact on sustainable energy supply and transformation. *Next Research, 1*(2), 100072. https://doi.org/https://doi.org/10.1016/j.nexres.2024.100072

Simon, P., & Gogotsi, Y. (2008). Materials for electrochemical capacitors. *Nat Mater, 7*(11), 845-854. https://doi.org/10.1038/nmat2297

Wu, X. (2023). Nanostructured Electrodes for High-Performance Supercapacitors and Batteries. *Nanomaterials, 13*, 2807. https://doi.org/10.3390/nano13202807

Yadlapalli, R. T., Alla, R. R., Kandipati, R., & Kotapati, A. (2022). Super capacitors for energy storage: Progress, applications and challenges. *Journal of Energy Storage, 49*, 104194. https://doi.org/https://doi.org/10.1016/j.est.2022.104194

Yang, B., Zhang, W., & Zheng, W. (2023). Unlocking the full energy densities of carbon-based supercapacitors. *Materials Research Letters, 11*(7), 517-546. https://doi.org/10.1080/21663831.2023.2183783

Zhang, L. L., & Zhao, X. S. (2009). Carbon-based materials as supercapacitor electrodes [10.1039/B813846J]. *Chemical Society reviews, 38*(9), 2520-2531. https://doi.org/10.1039/B813846J

CONTRIBUTORS

H.E. Dr. Chafik RACHADI,

Ambassador of His Majesty the King of Morocco to the Republic of Korea

H.E. Dr. Chafik Rachadi has been serving as the Ambassador of His Majesty the King of Morocco to the Republic of Korea since October 13, 2016. He was also elected Vice-President of the Korea-Arab Society (October 2022) and has served as the Dean of the Diplomatic Corps in Seoul and Dean of the African Group of Ambassadors since September 2024. His career spans decades of public service, including three terms as a Member of Parliament (2002–2016), during which he held the position of Vice-President of the Moroccan Parliament and led significant collaborations with international organizations such as the World Bank and the European Union. He also served as President of the Chamber of Commerce, Industry, and Services for four consecutive terms (2003–2015) and as First Vice-President of the Arab Labor Organization (2009–2011). H.E. Chafik Rachadi holds a doctorate in private law from Perpignan University, France, and advanced degrees in business administration, finance, and international management.

Brendan M. Howe (Ewha Womans University)

✉ bmg.howe@gmail.com

Brendan M. Howe (B.A. Hons Oxon, M.A. UKC, Ph.D. TCD) is Dean and Professor of the Graduate School of International Studies, Ewha Womans University, where he has worked since 2001. He served two terms as Associate Dean and two more as Department Chair. He currently serves as President of the *Asian Political and International Studies Association* and has been elected to serve as President of the *World International Studies Committee* from July 2025. From August 2025-August 2026 he will be supported by the *Alexander von Humboldt Foundation* for his sabbatical research at the University of Heidelberg. He has previously held research fellowships at the East-West Center in Honolulu (twice), the Freie Universität Berlin, the University of Sydney Center for International Security Studies, De La Salle University, Georgetown

University, and the Korea National Defense University. Previous academic employers include the University of Dublin, Trinity College, Universiti Malaysia Sarawak, and Beijing Foreign Studies University. His research focuses on human rights, security, and development, and their intersections in the nexuses of human security, international organization, and democratic governance. He has published around 150 related books, articles, and book chapters.

John Gyun Yeol Park (Gyeongsang National University)

📧 pgy556@gnu.kr

John Gyun Yeol Park is a professor in the Department of Ethics Education at Gyeongsang National University (GNU), Jinju, Republic of Korea. He has taught political philosophy or political ethics, such as North Korean Studies, International Affairs and Ethics, and National Security since 2007. Before joining GNU, he was a research fellow at the Korea National Defense University. He is the author of several books, including Community, Ethics and Security on the Korean Peninsula (Co-written in English), National Security and Moral Education (in Korean), Peace Security and Moral Education (in Korean), National Security and Military Ethics (in Korean), and others. His current research interests are political ethics and its evaluation. Now he is a president for Korea Association for Public Value which has published Journal of Public Value since June 2021.

Abdellah ACHACH (Researcher in International Law)

📧 achach.mxh@gmail.com

Dr. Abdellah Achach holds a Ph.D. in International Law from Mohammed V University, Rabat. Prior to his doctoral studies, he earned a Master's degree in international and diplomatic law from the same University and a Bachelor's degree in public law from Moulay Ismail University in Meknes. Dr. Achach also obtained a certificate from the Pakistan Foreign Service Academy (Islamabad) following in-depth training on the practice of international relations in addition to a certificate on diplomatic negotiations and Chinese foreign policy, organized in Shanghai by the China-Arab Center for Reform and Development. He also completed a one-year professional training on international relations and diplomacy at the Moroccan Academy of Diplomatic Studies in Rabat. Mr. Achach currently serves as the Economic

Counsellor at the Embassy of the Kingdom of Morocco in Seoul. He has previously served as Counsellor in the political section of the Embassy of Morocco in Beijing and Secretary of Foreign Affairs in the Asian Affairs Department at the Moroccan Ministry of Foreign Affairs in Rabat.

Jongnam Choi (Western Illinois University)

✉ choijnam@hotmail.com

Dr. Jongnam Choi is a Professor in the Department of Earth, Atmospheric, and Geographic Information Sciences at Western Illinois University. He teaches meteorology, climate change, and quantitative geography. His research interests emerge at the intersection of climate, weather, and human well-being. His recent research project includes climate changes in Northeast Asia and the impact of rainfall in subtropical forests using remotely sensed data and CO2 emission. He is an author/editor of atlases, books, and book chapters such as The Handy Weather Answer Book, The National Atlas of Korea, The Geography of Korea, and The Geography of Dokdo. He also contributes to many journals and encyclopedias.

Soonyoung Lee (Ret. Colonel)

Ret. Colonel, MSN. RN. Masters of Science in Nursing, Registered Nurse

✉ nurcaptain@gmail.com

She is a retired army colonel in the Republic of Korea and holds a Master of Science in Nursing. She graduated from the Korea Armed Forces Nursing Academy (KAFNA) and served as a nursing officer for 34 years. She lectured on nursing and served as the Chief of Teaching Division and the Director of the Military Nursing Research Institute at the KAFNA. Additionally, I worked as the Chief of Preventive Medicine at the Armed Forces Medical Command. After retirement, she has served as the Vice President of the Korean Coaching Association and the President of the Health Leaders Forum.

Hyoungbin Park (Seoul National University of Education)

✉ profphb@snue.ac.kr

She is a professor in the Department of Ethics Education at Seoul National University of Education (SNUE) in Seoul, Republic of Korea. As an accomplished author, she has written several works, including The Moral Intelligence Lesson (in Korean), AI Ethics, Neuroscience, and Education (in Korean), Theory and Practice of Moral Pedagogy (in Korean), the series If You Had to Choose, What Would You Do? (in Korean), Neuroscience and Moral Education (in Korean), Artificial Intelligence Ethics and Moral Education (in Korean), AI Era Transforming Education in Korea (in Korean), among others. Currently, she serves as the Chief of the SNUE Neuroethics Convergence Education Research Center (NCERC) and also as the Chief of the SNUE Value Ethics AI Hub Center (VEAHC). Her ongoing research interests span across Moral Psychology, Neuroethics, Reunification Education, Citizenship Education, and the Diagnosi of Morality.

Ho Jae Shin (Kongju National University)

✉ hjshin@kongju.ac.kr

Dr. Ho Jae Shin is a professor in the Department of Ethics Education at Kongju National University, where he teaches moral education, character education, and civic education. His academic interests lie in moral and political philosophy, as well as moral psychology, and he conducts research aimed at supporting the educational field. His key publications include *"A Study on the Framework Guiding the Direction of the National Character Education Policy"*, *"Exploring the Development and Issues of Representative and Participatory Democracy"*, and *"From Democratic Citizenship Education to Global Citizenship Education"*.

Nouha Benjelloun Andaloussi (Korea University)

✉ nbenjelloun05@gmail.com

She is a PhD candidate at Korea University specializing in international cooperation, with a focus on colonial studies. Her research examines colonial heritage in Casablanca and the role of citizen participation. She holds dual Master's degrees in International Sciences and Comparative Analysis of Mediterranean Societies from the University of Turin (Italy) and Mohammed VI Polytechnic University (Morocco).

Tim Cheongho Lee (Sangmyung University)

✉ humantad@hanmail.net

Dr. Tim Cheongho Lee graduated from Seoul National University with a B.A., M.A., and Ph.D. in Ethics Education. He continued his education in the United States, where he received a Ph.D. in Philosophy from Southern Illinois University (Carbondale) in 2018. Dr. Lee is currently employed at Sangmyung University in Seoul, Korea, where he pursues his research interests in American Pragmatism and AI Ethics. His academic trajectory demonstrates a commitment to contributing to the growing dialogue in the fields of American pragmatism and AI ethics.

Hyunsoo KIM (Pusan National University)

✉ hans.kim@pusan.ac.kr

Dr. Hyunsoo Kim is an Associate Professor in the Department of Ethics Education & Director of Graduate Program of International Education Development Cooperation Major at Pusan National University (PNU), Pusan, Republic of Korea. In 2002 he got his Ph. D. from Seoul National University, Korea. He has taught Applied Ethics such as Biomedical Ethics and AI Ethics, together with Moral Education curriculum and teaching & learning since 2019. Before joining PNU, he was a research fellow at the Korea Institute of Curriculum and Evaluation. He is the author of several books, including Biomedical Ethics, Marriage and Family Ethics, Business Ethics in Current Society, Contractualism and Deontology (all in Korean), and others. His Current research interests are International Relations, Applied Ethics especially on AI Ethics, Moral Psychology, Moral Education. Now he is an Editor in chief of Korea Association for Public Value which has published Journal of Public Value since June 2021.

Wonseok Bang (Gyeongsang National University)

✉ bangws@daum.net

Dr. Bang holds a doctorate in Business Administration from Gyeongsang National University and is currently a Research Professor at the Center for Entrepreneurship Studies. He earned a Master's degree in Business Administration from Sogang University and graduated from the Korea Air Force Academy. He is a member of the Jinju K-Entrepreneurship Committee (Present), a member of the Korean Institute for Global

Entrepreneurship Research (Present), and a vice president of the Korean Society for Safety Culture (Present). Major publications are as followings: *Entrepreneurship and Visionary Startups for Corporate Sustainability*, Pakyoungsa (2023), *Malvin Berkowitz's PRIMED Character Education Theory* (Co-author), Kyoyookgwahaksa (2024) etc.

Hongje Cho (Soongsil University)

✉ chj3050@naver.com

Dr. Hongje Cho is lecturer in law at Soongsil University, where he has worked since 2023. After he had finished Ph.D. degree in international law at the University of Kyungbook in 2001, he has served as an air force officer and researched at the Korea National Defense University (KNDU) for last twenty-nine years. While doing his Ph.D. degree, he majored International Law and International Relations. He researched at KNDU on North Korea Ballistic Missile, International Space Law and Nuclear issue, International Terrorism, Nuclear Summit Meeting, North Korea Space Launch and Capability, North Korea's UAV attack, North Korea's GPS Jamming, International law and legitimacy of Preemptive Strike on North Korea Nuclear facility. Also he researched as a visiting scholar at McGill University(Canada) from Dec 2012 to May 2013 and he joined as a visiting scholar at Elliott School of International Affairs at George Washington University from Dec 2017 to Jun 2018.

N. S. Reddy (Gyeongsang National University)

✉ nsreddy@gnu.ac.kr

Dr. Nagireddy Gari Subba Reddy (N. S. Reddy) is a Full Professor of Materials Science at Gyeongsang National University (GNU), Jinju, South Korea. He holds a Ph.D. in Computational Materials Science from IIT Kharagpur, India, along with degrees in Metallurgy, Mechanical Engineering, and diploma in Automobile Engineering. With nearly 90 Q1 and Q2 publications, he actively mentors students in research and thesis writing. His expertise spans Artificial Neural Networks (ANN), Explainable AI (XAI), and Machine Learning (ML), applied to high-entropy alloys, battery materials, diffusion prediction, corrosion modeling, sustainability, and healthcare. He has developed ANN-based sustainability analysis software, integrating prediction, sensitivity analysis, and variable optimization. His recent work extends ANN and

XAI to entrepreneurial marketing and social sciences. His current projects include sustainability modeling in nonprofit healthcare, AI-driven energy materials, creep rupture life prediction in steels, and Titanium alloy microstructure-property relationships. Actively collaborating across disciplines, he contributes to AI-driven materials research and industrial applications. Dr. Reddy has built a strong global research network through collaborations and academic visits to Hong Kong, Thailand, Malaysia, Taiwan, Singapore, Czech Republic, Germany, the UK, the US, and Japan, advancing AI, materials science, and sustainability.